Seeing the Joy in Affliction

Seeing the Joy in Affliction

◆

A UNIQUE CHRISTIAN VIEW OF SUFFERING

Michael Shelley

iUniverse, Inc.
New York Lincoln Shanghai

Seeing the Joy in Affliction
A UNIQUE CHRISTIAN VIEW OF SUFFERING

All Rights Reserved © 2004 by Michael L. Shelley

No part of this book may be reproduced or transmitted in any form or by any means, graphic, electronic, or mechanical, including photocopying, recording, taping, or by any information storage retrieval system, without the written permission of the publisher.

iUniverse, Inc.

For information address:
iUniverse, Inc.
2021 Pine Lake Road, Suite 100
Lincoln, NE 68512
www.iuniverse.com

Bible quotes designated as "KJV" are from *The New Scofield Reference Bible, Authorized King James Version,* Oxford University Press, New York, 1967.

Bible quotes designated as "NAS" are taken from the NEW AMERICAN STANDARD BIBLE®, Copyright © 1960, 1962, 1963, 1968, 1971, 1972, 1973, 1975, 1977, 1995, by The Lockman Foundation. Used by permission.

ISBN: 0-595-32857-1

Printed in the United States of America

To the memory of my father, Aubrey Shelley, who experienced much affliction in his life and with whom I never had the opportunity to share this book. I rejoice with him now as he stands in the very Presence of our blessed Savior.

Contents

Preface .... *xi*

Chapter 1   Unleashing God's power to see His purpose in affliction (a personal experience) 1

   Introduction 1

   Affliction will come 3

   The initial blessing of affliction 6

   Afflictions prepare us for more affliction 8

   Affliction enables new ministry 11

Chapter 2   Why does physical and emotional suffering come to God's children? 19

   Why is there Suffering in the Body of Christ? 19

   What does God intend when His children suffer? 24

Chapter 3   Using affliction to minister outside the Body of Christ 34

Chapter 4   Using affliction to minister within the Body of Christ 41

   Emphasizing the importance of intimate praise 42

   Ministering to those in affliction 48

   The question of "faith" 51

Chapter 5   A word on "healing"—the different views 57

Chapter 6   Moving toward His appointed ministry for you within times of affliction 82

	The on-going search for ministry: Assessing our appointed place	84
	It's the Fruit; not the Assessment	88
Chapter 7	Expecting and desiring God's continued work in growing your ministry (The blessing of affliction)	97
	Purpose in our affliction	98
	Boldness in our appointed ministry	102
	The problem of physical affliction (healing from disease)	104
	It's still a battle—expect it!	106
	Rejoice always	108
Epilogue		111

Acknowledgements

I wish to thank my loving wife who bore these trials with me, encouraged me in my walk with the Lord, and confirmed for me what the Lord was teaching me. I thank my children, Maria, Andrew, and Josh, who love the Lord and never stopped rejoicing with me as we faced emotional trials knowing we were in God's Sovereign Hand.

I appreciate my Sunday School class who allowed me to teach scripture each Sunday from the perspective expressed in this book. John and Nina Bowser, Gene and Joan Chenoweth, Bill and Betty Dean, Beau Dodge, De Gaskins, Bettina Smiley, and Phil and Arlene Smith all helped me to refine this message by challenging and confirming my teaching. Great thanks to Bill Dean for his thorough editing of the work.

Finally, I wish to thank the faithful reviewers of this work who took on the challenge of critical review, holding me true to the scriptures, correcting me, and encouraging me. Special thanks to Pastor Stan Tharp, Pastor Tom Dallis, Pastor Mike Owen, Jim Altensee, Marge David, Bill and Betty Dean, John and Nina Bowser, Paul and Trissa King, Sue Ray, and Sherry Shelley.

Preface

I have taken on the writing of this manuscript because I feel the Lord has shown me something new and fresh that He wants all Christians to understand. It derives from my personal experience with physical affliction—primarily, terminal brain cancer. My experience in the midst of this disease has been completely different from anything I ever imagined it might be if I were ever faced with it.

The Lord has granted me numerous opportunities to speak of these things with fellow believers, with unbelieving friends, and with several church and fellowship groups. I made journal notations about the experience on a daily basis. I eventually came to the point where I had a central message that I wanted everyone to hear and which I spoke in various forms at hour-long seminars as the Lord gave opportunity. Eventually it occurred to me that I had a message that might be presented in the form of a book.

Soon after this notion occurred to me, my pastor was interviewing me in preparation for my speaking during an upcoming sermon. He mentioned off-hand that I might consider writing a book. I reasoned to myself that I would need a couple of months off from work to take on the effort. A few weeks later, I was laid off from work for a set 2-month period. So, I am placing finger to keyboard to see if the Lord will bless the effort. I have no idea or particular vision for how the Lord will use this. I do not know if it will ever make print or how it might be distributed. But I am moving forward in obedience to what I feel the Lord is laying before me.

I am a university professor in a graduate engineering school and have written several articles for science and engineering journals. I am not a Christian writer, and my name is not generally known among believers as a speaker or other minister. Therefore, I need to offer some explanation of my credentials.

I have grown up and have continued in churches of the conservative-evangelical-protestant bent during my 50 years. I have read the Bible through several times, and I have taught an adult Sunday School class or home-based Bible study continuously for the past 30 years as I have lived in many different cities and attended many different churches. I am a layman with experience in church ministry and with a particular experience in physical affliction that the Lord has given me to share. Therefore, I ask for grace and understanding from the reader and that this be taken as one person's experience that I hope will help you in your pursuit of God as He leads you.

Finally, there is much that I have to say about how we should respond to affliction that will seem contrary to the practice of many of my dear Christian brothers and sisters. Specifically, this book does not teach that we should regard all physical affliction as contrary to God's perfect Will nor that we should, therefore, claim by faith a promise of physical healing in every case. I attempt to approach this more definitively by devoting a chapter to these issues. It is not my intent to argue or to bring any debate that is not edifying. If the appearance is otherwise, then I hope my fellow Christians will feel free to approach me on these issues as the Lord may lead.

I pray that God will place this book in the hands of those He wishes to read it, and that He will bless you as you read and apply it to your life under His Sovereign Hand.

Mike Shelley
February 2004

1

Unleashing God's power to see His purpose in affliction (a personal experience)

Introduction

In September 2002 at the age of 50, I was diagnosed with terminal brain cancer (*Glioblastoma Multi Forme*, to be exact). I had one child who had started a career and two children still in college. My wife and I were looking forward to future retirement years and what we might be doing with that time. Suddenly, those thoughts were gone, there was serious concern about my children finishing college as planned, and there were serious concerns as to whether I had adequately prepared for my surviving wife in the wake of my untimely death. There was initial brain surgery followed by massive radiation therapy, and I now still struggle through chemotherapy with a few more months to go.

I think all of us wonder at one time or another how we would respond to these kinds of circumstances, assuming (and hoping) it will never really happen to us. My experience has been completely different from what I had imagined. I declare without reservation that this has been the very best time of my life. This has nothing to do with "appreciating life" now that I'm told that I don't have much of it left. This has to do with the new and fresh and wonderful things the Lord has done in my life through this affliction. This statement immediately raises questions in the minds of many Christian believers. Many would say that God never intends for His children to suffer physically and emotionally under the oppression of this kind of disease. I write this book to tell a different story based on my personal experience. My intent is to bring encouragement to many in the Body of Christ, whether they feel they are currently suffering or not. I want others to understand the *blessing* of affliction when we are in the Lord and to have a joyful expectation of what the Lord intends to do with our affliction. **And He does have wonderful intentions!** It has been a challenge to keep up with everything the Lord has brought into my life through this experience, and I learned early-on to journal daily. The book is based on that journaling and gives a personal account (by example) of what the Lord has done in my life through this affliction as well as expounding on the general principles I believe are evident for everyone.

My entire motivation for writing this book comes from the experience that I document in this chapter. I have never suffered a great deal in my life, even as I write this. But my experiences of the past 3 years are clearly significant and qualify as real afflictions by most peoples' standards, although I clearly have not suffered as much as many. I am well educated but not in the theological disciplines. My understanding of scripture, the principles of the Faith, and spiritual things in general arise from very strong campus discipleship ministries as a young Christian, my continual involvement in leadership and in various ministries within the church (including primarily adult teaching), and my personal worship and study before the Lord. My primary credentials for writing about affliction are simply that I have moved through these experiences with a God-granted grace that has brought powerful change to my life, and this has brought encouragement and teaching to me and to many people who have heard me speak and who have sought my counsel. My experience starts out like many others but takes a turn along the way that was unexpected and wonderful.

Affliction will come

Just over four years ago (Fall 1999) I was a very vibrant and healthy person. I was successful at work and involved in several ministries within the church. Family life was good, and I kept myself in good physical condition, running 25 miles per week and lifting very heavy (265 lbs) on the flat bench (not bad for a small 50 year old guy). I had a good view of myself and saw myself as being vibrant well into later years. I was the typical middle class American Christian, successful in work and struggling to balance work, family, and the discipleship disciplines we all feel is important to growing in the faith (daily quiet time, study in the Word, adequate prayer life, etc).

In November of 1999 I suddenly lost the ability to exercise. Overnight (without realizing it until I arrived at the gym) I was only able to sustain a single set of 5 lifts at 185 lbs and was then exhausted, unable to continue any workout and staggering to a chair, when I would normally sustain an upper body lifting work out for over an hour. It took me 30 minutes to recover. Not knowing what was wrong (this wasn't just an occasional "bad day"), I decided to run instead, and I stretched out to prepare for a 5 mile set. After a quarter mile I collapsed and required another 30 minutes to recover. This was the only symptom that was evident. My life otherwise was not affected—I simply could not tolerate any exercise when I tried. This condition sustained at that level for 2 ½ years while I began to gain weight and struggled with diet issues that I never had to struggle with before. Several medical specialists could find no diagnostic pathway to even begin to explain the condition.

After a while, chronic fatigue and depression issues began to arise as part of this affliction. My dear wife, Sherry, was barely able to hang on amidst my irritability and her trying to fill the gaps I was leaving in the home as husband and father. I became very disillusioned concerning my ministry and place in the Body of Christ. I was involved in teaching Sunday School, facilitating within the discipleship outreach ministry, leading in the choir, part of the prayer ministry and congregational support ministries, as well as food distribution ministries within community outreach. I was very busy but was having a very hard time seeing any real substantive ministry taking place. Amidst my depression and fatigue, I systematically dropped out of all of these ministries (even when it let people down). I was tired, discouraged, and depressed. I kept only my position as adult Sunday School teacher (not wanting to completely drop away), feeling that whatever the Lord wanted to reveal to me concerning my ministry would come through that means if anything. But even that became worse as I eventually surrendered to a practice of getting up at 4:30 every Sunday morning to begin to try and throw together something half-way decent. Relationships became frayed and, in a few cases, significantly damaged. The psychiatrist said I was not clinically depressed but had most of the symptoms. No chemical therapy had any effect. I felt I was in a pretty dark place.

I began putting fewer and fewer hours in at work (cutting from 60 to 45 hours per week). For the first time in my career, I almost got into real trouble due to productivity. I was a college professor, and the State of Ohio had granted me a lot of money for a project that I had successfully completed, but I couldn't muster up the energy or will to complete the large final report. When the report was 3–4 months overdue, the State finally had to jump on me. (The associate dean immediately informed me that the dean, my boss, was the chairman of the regional committee responsible for seeing that these kinds of reports were submitted on time!). The report was finally completed, but I had almost seriously embarrassed my organization and had almost come into personal ill repute. (In the end, there were no negative repercussions; the Lord protected my reputation).

The initial blessing of affliction

One night as I was downstairs in the basement (in my quiet place where everyone knows not to disturb me), I pondered where I was and what was happening. I realized that the Lord had been showing me a lot of things that I would not have otherwise seen had I not gone through this hard time. Among them were:

1. I am a critical part of my wife's spiritual growth and must be devoted to her in that regard (I saw the effects of not being her help-mate).

2. I was so busy in various ministries within the church that I was not allowing the Lord to show me what my appointed ministry is.

3. Proper relationships are essential to any ministry no matter what that ministry may be. I can no longer use my introverted personality as an explanation for why I am not called to a ministry. I am called to relate and to grow in how I relate to the brethren in order to minister.

When I realized that the Lord was using my struggle to show me these kinds of things and to begin freeing me toward new and effectual ministry, **_I decided to simply thank Him and praise Him for the hardship_**. I spent 20–30 minutes just praising Him for His wisdom and His work in my life, bowing before Him and just desiring His Presence!

From that moment on, I was completely free from the fatigue and depression symptoms (and they have never returned). Sherry was overjoyed, and our marriage relationship began to grow in a way it never had before. Relationships were restored at church. I had renewed energy at work ("a new man", according to my colleagues). I began to receive new vision concerning how the Lord wanted to bless my ministry within the Body. I began to journal about what the Lord was showing me daily, and my personality actually began to change in areas and in ways suited to ministries the Lord was placing before me (my Meyers-Briggs personality scores were literally changing; I was becoming a more "*sensitive*" person). All this I experienced while I daily spent 20 minutes every morning in pure praise before the Lord (no confession, no thanking for things, no petition [these were reserved for other prayer times]; just praise), and ending with thanking Him for the hardships of the past and the present. I still had no exercise tolerance; He wouldn't let me back in the gym. (I stopped concerning myself about that after a while because I knew the Lord was dealing with some pride issues there. Besides, the gym was not a place I needed to be with all the vanity and the women dressed the way they were; and all that time spent running should be used more effectively.)

This was a huge revival in my life that the Lord had chosen to bless me with through the afflictions of taking away physical strength and endurance and allowing the affliction of fatigue and depression. And the revival sustained because I was thanking Him for the affliction and praising Him daily. ***I have come to really believe that anyone not entering into pure praise everyday (allowing Him to fill your heart to a point that it overflows with praise) is foundationally deficient in ministry, whatever one's ministry might be***.

Afflictions prepare us for more affliction

This experience in affliction was used by God to really bless my life, and it also prepared me for the ***next*** affliction, for it was in the midst of this revival that the cancer issue arose. Its discovery was completely fortuitous (I had no symptoms suggesting cancer). I was simply disengaging from the doctors on the exercise intolerance issue, being satisfied that they had done all they could do and really were not getting anywhere. I told them that the only thing I was not satisfied with was the neurological workup and that I would like some imaging performed (I was looking for signs of minor stroke that might not be otherwise outwardly evident). The doctor decided to write the order (to accommodate the patient's desires) but felt sure the radiologist would not accept the order because there was no real foundation for the request. He did accept the order, however, and I had the MRI performed on September 11, 2002. As I was attempting to leave, a technician ran out and asked me to wait in the lobby; the radiologist wanted me to see a doctor before leaving. Within 20 minutes, a doctor was explaining that a golf-ball-sized mass was found in the center of my head (beneath the right frontal lobe just above the optic nerve). That afternoon, the surgeon was explaining what he was seeing on the image. He had "seen this kind of thing before". He offered 3 or 4 explanations of what it could be, all of which were not immediately dangerous. He did not suspect a malignancy. The advice was to wait for 2 months and image again to note any changes and make decisions from there. I immediately rejected that advice and opted for immediate surgery (God's prompting, I believe).

I was on the table one week later, and, when the surgeon saw the mass with his own eyes, he immediately realized his misjudgment (and pathology confirmed). Had I followed his advice and done nothing for 2 months, I would not have survived to make the MRI appointment. The diagnosis was "Glioblastoma Multi-Forme", a very high grade malignancy. The surgeon removed essentially all of the visible mass, but the diagnosis was a death sentence. A few days later, Sherry and I sat in the surgeon's office to receive the definitive discussion. I was waiting for a complex presentation of probabilities for this risk group versus that risk group and multiple selections of possible survival rates that I would have to somehow package in my mind to make some sense of it. But it wasn't that way at all. The prognosis was clear and simple. I would undergo massive radiation therapy followed by possible forms of chemotherapy (limited). There might come a time when the renewed tumor could again be at least partially operable. But considering all this, I was to die within 11 months (not "one year", but 11 months!). In the words of this surgeon, "I have never seen anyone survive this condition in my entire career."

This was a prognosis I could understand and deal with. I appreciated the clarity and was amazed at how the Lord was present and blessed me at that moment. I was freshly accustomed to seeing God work through adversity according to His good purposes (in the midst of the first affliction of depression and fatigue), and my thoughts immediately went to the question of what the Lord intended to do with this. I never once (and have never since) felt any dread or disappointment or emotional despair over the cancer prognosis. In fact, the surgeon became concerned, apparently feeling that I hadn't understood him or was in psychotic denial. Within a couple of minutes I was asking trivial questions about post surgical recovery and was not behaving like his other patients suddenly confronted with such news. I was completely protected by God's Hand resting upon me and allowing me to see beyond the nature of the affliction itself.

I accepted the recommended radiation and chemotherapy, judging them to be conventionally appropriate within the medical community. One must live honorably before God and before men, and I felt that accepting the conventional treatments was the right behavior before my family and others. It also offered the best opportunity (medically) to survive the full 11 months, giving sufficient time to "put my affairs in order"—another important responsible behavior. (I would avoid looking for exotic and experimental treatments in a desperate attempt to squeeze out a few more months of life. This would not be honorable behavior, and I knew that God would have me focus my attention on other, more significant endeavors.) Having made these decisions, I felt a peace about the circumstances and focused on receiving what the Lord wanted to do in my life with this situation.

Affliction enables new ministry

I continued to praise and thank God everyday (and now I had something new to thank Him for!). The things that He was building spiritually in me up to that point now had opportunity to be built in practice. The ministry opportunities that came with the prognosis were overwhelming:

1. Among unbelievers, when you are dying, and they know you're dying, and they know you don't have a problem with it, and, not only that, but you're more than willing to talk about it, (guess what!) they want to talk about it! Everyday I have had colleagues come in and out of my office to "pay respects" and see how I am handling the concept of death. Once we get past the initial awkwardness (about 30 seconds) and they know it's OK to talk openly, I have an opportunity to talk about the way the Lord has blessed through this affliction and what a joy I am experiencing. I can then talk about what I am looking forward to regardless of the outcome. I have had the opportunity to share the

gospel virtually unchallenged (because I'm "dying") to so many people that I have lost count.

2. I've had several opportunities to minister to groups of believers. When I briefly shared with a member of a Christian fellowship group within my organization, he suggested that I come and talk to the group about these things. I shared with this group for an hour about the things I'm presenting here. It prompted significant discussion and became an example of the kind of sharing they wanted their group to have. I was drawn into their prayer group and have been able to minister to a lot of prayer needs on a weekly basis by simply relating my experience to the challenges in other men's lives. The chaplain in my organization invited me to speak at the Gospel Service on base (I work on a military installation). The day I went to speak, the church was packed. He gave me his pulpit for 20 minutes. Scores of people wanted to greet me and hug me at the end, many declaring that they realized now that God was trying to bless and strengthen through many of their adversities, and they were trying to rebuke them and throw them off. The chaplain said that the congregation was still talking about it the following week. I have had several opportunities to speak at my own church, and God has added His blessing to every opportunity.

3. Another amazing thing is the ministry opportunities among individual believers, and their ministry to me.

I really enjoy sharing these things with believers and seeing them rejoice with me (a new concept of ministry the Lord opened for me). It seemed that everyday (at work, at church, in other environments) the Lord would place before me a brother or sister in the Lord who was struggling through some kind of ordeal. I rarely had "the answer" to the questions they posed, but I seemed to have a new heart for listening and empathizing with them. And even though I couldn't professionally counsel them through their individual struggle, what I always shared was that no matter what the struggle, the Lord has wonderful purposes in mind for his children in the affliction; and when we praise Him and thank Him for that fact, we are in a better position to receive the blessing. This has always been the point of ministry that they seemed to need, and virtually all of them have approached me later and told me of their own wonderful experience in receiving what the Lord had for them in the affliction after they gave thanks and praised Him for it.

4. Finally, new ministry opportunities did not stop with me. The Lord exploded into the life of my entire family. It seems that my prior short-comings in worship and ministry was a hindrance to what the Lord intended for my wife and children. My children (who all loved the Lord and sought His Will in their lives) suddenly experienced deliverance from many hindrances in their relationship with the Lord and in specific ministries. My wife, Sherry, had been struggling

with apparent closed doors in the area of ministry she desired (worship & music). Now, as we began praying together with an enlightened perspective on how the Lord uses adversity, the Lord began to bear fruit in her in the area of prayer. The Lord brought many before her who had real needs, and she was especially anointed by God to effectually pray for them in their circumstances. Many were delivered from hindrances in their lives through her ministry. I remember visiting in the hospital intensive care unit and seeing Sherry drawn to other patients in the room to pray for them. People around me (believers and non-believers) commented to me about the very real effect they could see in those people as a result of her prayers. The Lord revealed a new and effectual ministry within her that I believe was released when we came together in praise over my affliction (which, in reality, was her affliction as well). I am fully convinced that praise is the starting point for seeing the ministry that *God* intends us to have. (I will deal with this more later). During one weekend when I was speaking at all four of our church's services about the joy in my life as a result of this affliction, the pastor remarked to me privately between services that it blessed him to see *the joy on Sherry's face as I spoke, giving all appearance that she was right there with me in the same place.* I am amazed at the dimensions of God's Grace in the midst of what I am going through, *as well as the new understanding of the significance of the role of husband and father!* (This is an issue that I can't begin to address completely in this book. It has been my experience that ministry opportunity and effectiveness outside the home grows from ministry within the home. I am convicted that I will not even begin to see the fullness of the Lord's ministry in my life until I allow His anointing in my life to pour out fully on my wife and children. I hope that my learning in this area will grow to the point of desiring to write a book on this subject.)

But what amazes me even more is what other believers say they see *in me*! So many believers have talked about how I have "changed", that there is a "spirit of peace" about me, that they "see a glow on me", or that they sense God's Presence. I don't know what they are talking about. I've been ministered to by people who seem to have the Presence of God abiding on them. I assumed those people knew that about themselves and understood that that particular anointing was on them and part of their ministry in the Body. But now people are saying this about me, and I don't sense anything different. It is apparently an anointing the Lord gives at His pleasure that has nothing to do with me.

I had a long conversation with the organizational chaplain one day before the invitation to speak at his service. We talked about my condition and what the Lord was doing in it. When we finished our conversation, he said that I had brought him significant teaching that day. He then asked me to speak at a couple of groups and also at his chapel service (the Gospel Service mentioned above). I asked him to please give me guidance on the direction he'd like me to take in each case so I could focus and be respectful of the time. He immediately said, "No, that's not the point. Say whatever you want. Just come and talk to the people. I want them to see the Peace of God that I see on you, and I wish I had that peace." The chaplain's words humbled and mystified me (absolutely blew me away!). At his church, an elderly gentleman came and hugged me after the service. He said, "When I saw you sitting over there before the service, I turned to my wife and said, 'I sense the Presence of God on that man'." What an amazing blessing to hear those words!

Here is a portion of one of my personal journal entries a little over one month after my surgery:

> **The news of the prognosis spread very quickly, and many people came to visit. They were all amazed at the peace that seemed to surround me (even though I was never much aware of it). Ministry opportunities came from everywhere, both within the church and especially at work. Praising Him continues to grow and there is a new blessing to talk about almost every day (when my time with Him in praise and worship is maintained). Sherry and I are growing closer, believing we are being prepared for ministry (even though Sherry, of course, struggles emotionally with the prevailing medical prognosis). _This is the most blessed_**

time of my life! (from October 29, 2002 personal journal entry)

I did nothing to merit the blessings of this affliction, but it does seem that God chose to pour Himself out on me when I began praising and thanking and rejoicing <u>for</u> the affliction (not in spite of it). *Focusing on continually asking the Lord to relieve me of the affliction would have missed the mark.* This has been a foundational part of what the Lord has given me to speak and write about. But my experience in these things is much richer than what is expressed here. I have grown into a new *<u>intimacy</u>* with the Lord that is the source of a new joy and a new ministry anointing. I hope to adequately deal with these issues as we proceed.

As of this writing, I am still terminally ill with expected life measured in months. However, I have lived with no visible recurrence of the cancer for 6 months beyond the initial 11 month prognosis. We will talk about the whole concept of physical healing in later chapters.

◆ ◆ ◆

Questions for Meditation or Group Discussion

1. In the story told in this chapter, I sensed why the Lord had allowed my depression and physical weakness to develop before I began rejoicing in them (this was the initial motivation for praise). Later, with the cancer, I was able to immediately praise Him in this affliction without knowing what wonderful thing He might do. What does this say about the requirements God places on us to experience His full blessings, and what does this say about God's mercy toward us? Do you think it was God's perfect Will that I understand it first in the case of the depression, or was God just being merciful to me in my disobedience? If there is always one thing that is important for us to understand in our afflictions, what is it?

2. This chapter makes the statement that pure intimate praise is foundational (necessary) to realizing the full potential for ministry that God has placed in each of us. This kind of praise is difficult to describe. How would you describe it, either from your own experience or from how you would envision it for yourself? How would you practically approach beginning to make this a regular part of your spiritual growth (daily worship)? Would it likely be different for each person?

2

Why does physical and emotional suffering come to God's children?

I have had the opportunity to speak at churches and fellowship groups over the past year or so (because of my terminal condition and my response to it), with much experience in speaking to people afterwards about their specific concerns. I also teach an adult Sunday School class at my church in which much of the on-going teaching over the past year has been on this subject (it is a lively and talkative class). These discussions have brought more clearly to light the kinds of questions that are really on most peoples' minds.

Why is there Suffering in the Body of Christ?

The most fundamental question, of course, is "why". Why does God allow His children to suffer? Why do many suffer so much more than others? Why, when we pray for healing of our friends in church, do we often not seem to see God respond? Doesn't God want everyone to be healed? After all, aren't we commanded to pray for the sick? Why do some die in spite of our prayers? Did we not have enough faith?

We will talk later about whether or not these are appropriate questions to ask or whether God will ever answer them to our satisfaction before we see Him in glory. But, for now, they are common questions that deserve a rational response. I sat down with a military chaplain not long ago (my first encounter with my organizational chaplain mentioned in chapter 1). I was there on other business, but he soon recognized me as "the terminal cancer guy", and he closed the door for a 2 hour discussion. During our talk, he spoke of his frustration over this whole question of suffering in the Church. We are promised, of course, that suffering is part of being in Christ, but we usually think of this as some form of persecution because we declare the Name of Jesus and bear the cultural consequences (and most of us in the United States often feel guilty that we don't seem to be experiencing much of that). But what about random disease and sickness?

Now, this chaplain was not a young military officer fresh out of seminary but a seasoned 53 year old with 25 years of pastoral experience both in and out of the military. The types of congregations he pastored generally expected him to speak against all such disease in the Name of Jesus, rebuking the Enemy (Satan) for the attack, and claiming victory over the affliction. But, over many years of experience that included many miraculous healings, he was growing weary over a repeated scenario of no healing. The scenario would go something like this: A faithful sister within the church would be suddenly stricken with terminal illness. The pastor and congregation would declare healing for her in Jesus' Name, and they would fast and pray for her for months while her condition grew worse. Finally the ambulance would come to take her to the hospital. While being loaded into the ambulance she would look up at the pastor, shake her fist at the Enemy, and boldly declare that the Enemy would not get the victory. She would pass into the arms of the Lord two days later while in intensive care.

The chaplain was not expressing discouragement or any degree of doubt in the power of prayer. He had simply come to a point in his ministry where he felt a need to re-evaluate his understanding of God's purposes in affliction and exactly what it meant to pray in Jesus' Name (a subject we will touch on later). As we sat and talked, we agreed on two things:

First, the Enemy does attack God's children and has the desire and power to bring physical disease. In such cases, the mature believer should recognize the attack and stand against it in Jesus' Name. We should grow to the point that we are accustomed to taking authority over those things for which God has given us authority ("Resist the devil and he will flee from you." *James 4:7, NAS*). We are bought by His Blood, and we belong to Him. Therefore, we can effectively refuse to grant Satan any influence over our bodies and minds in instances of clear attack. A friend of mine, Sue, has a history of migraine headaches. She describes how she feels one coming on only when the Lord has laid a ministry opportunity before her and she is stepping out in obedience to minister. Left unchallenged, this attack would grow to completely debilitate her and prevent effective ministry. She has learned, however, to recognize that this is a specific attack of the Enemy to thwart God's will and direction in her life at specific moments. She knows now, through experience, that immediately standing against the attack in the Name of Jesus renders the attack ineffective, and the headache quickly subsides. Then great testimonies ensue from the work God has laid before her. In my friend's case, she was able to see a specific attack in specific moments. I have no doubt that there are other cases where the Enemy is attacking more subtly in our lives, perhaps in ways more difficult to call out directly and recognize. But in each such case, the Enemy would be acting by design to thwart our specific appointed ministry. It is this hindering that the mature believer would recognize as the hand of the Enemy. I suspect, however, that many of us can't recognize this because we pose no particular ministry threat to the Enemy and there really is no attack in progress. This leads to the second point the chaplain and I agreed on.

Secondly (we agreed), most physical affliction is not of this sort and is not dealt with by claiming victory over the Enemy. The simple fact is that we live in a corrupted creation that awaits complete redemption upon the return of our Lord. Our physical bodies (and minds) are part of that corrupted nature. We struggle to be renewed in our minds (to be one with God's heart and His thoughts concerning us) while our bodies are subject to the consequences of the environment we are a part of. Certainly, there are many life style behaviors that bring certain diseases that are less prevalent within the Body of Christ. But beyond that, I don't see any fewer afflictions within the church than I see outside the church. Furthermore, although I am personally aware of many instances of miraculous healing, diseases usually run their full course in Christians just like non-Christians; and, in the case of terminal illness, Christians die at an "untimely" time of life, just like non-Christians. We will look at the subject of healing and God's promises in that regard in the chapter on healing. For now, however, it is difficult for me to believe that all these faithful Christians met an untimely death because someone wasn't praying hard enough or someone didn't have enough faith to claim God's promises. When I see the manner in which many of these saints of God have met their death and the lives they have touched within that experience, it is clear to me that God's Presence was full in their lives. **The difference between the believer and the non-believer is not that one repels, rebukes, and avoids the affliction while the other, having no authority, succumbs to it. The difference is in how we move through the experience. The child of God expresses joyful ministry in full confidence of the Lord's Sovereign Hand (even in death) while the one still in darkness is defeated amidst a myriad of unanswered questions about "why".** This is the nature of the world we live in, and this is what sets Christians apart and even provides a basis for ministry. Anyone who sees the believer suffer through affliction in the joy of God's Presence will be drawn to what that believer has, even though it isn't understood.

So, my chaplain friend and I agreed on the above two points. But my recent experience leads me to believe that God, by His Hand and by His specific design, many times allows affliction to come to His children for His wonderful and gracious purposes. This was a difficult suggestion for my chaplain friend and is initially difficult for most Christians with whom I talk, but it is usually much easier to swallow after I relate my personal experience in my affliction and what the Lord has done within it. You can form your own judgment on how and why afflictions come as you read through this book, if you think it is edifying to ponder it. In the end, I think it is of little consequence how we choose to word these things ("the devil does it", "God does it", "it's the world we live in"…). Ultimately, God clearly "allows" His children to suffer, and we are promised that all these things work together for our good (*Rom 8:28)*. Seeking Him and finding that "good" purpose is what is important. Why do God's children suffer by affliction? Because, God intends wonderful things in them, and they are causes for joy when we understand that.

What does God intend when His children suffer?

If we accept that God allows affliction to come upon His children as part of His divine plan for our growth and ministry, we need to form an accurate expectation of what His intentions are and to realize how we need to respond.

First, we must realize that we will ultimately be with Him in perfect peace and joy surrounded by His glory for eternity and that any amount of suffering in this world is insignificant by comparison (*Rom 8:18*). This is the primary tool the Christian has in forming the right perspective—God has already won the total victory on our behalf and He has an unchangeable inheritance awaiting us shortly.

Second we must understand that, although we often must bear the consequences on earth for our sin, affliction for the child of God is not a punishment for anyone involved (our atonement is already achieved). Furthermore, He doesn't allow these afflictions just so we can appreciate our ultimate inheritance that much more (we will need no training to know full and complete joy when we enter His Presence).

Finally, affliction is more than just a set of circumstances within which we can display God's peace to the world around us. We must understand that God intends to do something new and fresh in our lives through the experience. He always wants to move us from where we are now to new levels of knowing Him and new levels of ministry. At times, this involves disciplining us concerning specific sin in our lives.

Paul speaks of this in 1 Corinthians 12 where he explains why some of us are sick:

> **Therefore whoever eats the bread and drinks the cup of the Lord in an unworthy manner, shall be guilty of the body and the blood of the Lord. But a man must examine himself, and in so doing he is to eat of the bread and drink of the cup. For he who eats and drinks, eats and drinks judgment to himself if he does not judge the body rightly. For this reason many among you are weak and sick, and a number sleep. But if we judged ourselves rightly, we would not be judged. But when we are judged, we are disciplined by the Lord so that we will not be condemned along with the world.**
>
> *(1 Cor 12: 27-32, NAS)*

This discipline is intended for good and, like other kinds of affliction the Lord allows, carries the purpose of bringing us more into Him and into His love in order to find our appointed place of ministry. We must expect that and enable it by a proper response. Let's look at a couple of examples from scripture on how God uses affliction, one which does not seem to be a case of disciplining, and one which does.

Job

Any discussion of suffering will usually involve a reference to Job. In this case, Satan was mounting an attack on Job's faithfulness in general with explicit permission from the Lord (*Job 1 and 2*). In fact, it appears that the Lord specifically invited Satan's attack by drawing specific attention to Job (*Job 1:8, 2:3*). The Lord was in sovereign control, limiting Satan's authority over Job's life and, ultimately, allowing Satan full reign short of actually killing him (*Job 1:12, 2:6*). Within this very broad boundary, the Enemy took everything—his children, his possessions, and his physical health. Job's physical suffering alone (as we read in the latter part of chapter 2) is something we could not even begin to comprehend. Amidst this, Job even had to endure some very bad counsel and accusations from his friends as well as encouragement from his wife to curse God and die!

What was God's intention in allowing this man of God to suffer in such a horrendous way? Was God trying to teach Job to take authority over the Enemy and declare his healing? The resolution of the book would suggest otherwise (*Job 42*). Was God punishing Job for unrighteousness (as Job's counselors insisted)? On the contrary, Job's faithfulness and integrity was phenomenal as he declared God's sovereignty ("'Shall we indeed accept good from God and not accept adversity?' In all this Job did not sin with his lips." *Job 2:10*). Was God trying to prove something to Satan (as the opening dialog might initially suggest to us)? Again, it is clear in the course of the book that this is not the case. God does not answer to Satan, and He never returns to address Satan in the end. Was God placing Job in a situation where Job could ask all the questions we all would ask in such circumstances so that He could provide the answers for us? Job asked these questions, and God never answered them. God had something else in mind.

Job's friends could not lay any specific charge against him, and Job (in response to his friends' ceaseless counsel) defends his integrity. Yet, Job does express a lack of understanding of God's purposes and expresses a desire for an opportunity to plead his case before God; but he can't do so because there is no *"mediator" (Job 9: 32-35)*. Finally, a fourth counselor suddenly is revealed who speaks more to the Truth of the circumstances *(Job 32-37)*. Job does not have any direct response to Elihu's dissertation, and his heart is prepared to experience God Himself. God comes to Job directly (without a mediator) and confronts Job with His very Nature and Being. In God's Presence, Job's questions (which were never answered) fall away *(Job 38-41)*. Job is awe-stricken before God as he is "blessed" with a new and fresh vision of who God is *(Job 40:3-5; 42:1-6)*. And here we see God fulfilling His purposes in Job through this affliction, as initially demonstrated in Job's ministry to his 3 friends *(Job 42:8-10)*. What a blessing this must have been to Job and many others around him as he most certainly must have taught and testified of the Lord's Hand in his life, moving him into new understanding and relationship through affliction and, finally, restoring him and blessing him far beyond what he had before *(Job 42:12-17)*. This was clearly God's intention from the beginning—using the Enemy, using the corruption of creation, and using the corrupt counsel of his friends to bring Job from the place where he was to a new place of understanding and ministry. I believe that every time a child of God suffers, we can declare God's wonderful intent in these terms.

Jonah

Jonah is another interesting example of God's purposes fulfilled through affliction of His children. When Jonah received God's call to go to Nineveh with a message of repentance and he responded by traveling in the opposite direction (*Jonah 1:1-3*), he wasn't "afraid" to go to Nineveh, he wasn't running from God, and he wasn't just immature and learning how to be an obedient prophet. Jonah was an anointed prophet to God's people, and He was accustomed to speaking God's Word boldly. The fact is he simply did not want the people of Nineveh to hear a message of repentance because he did not want them to repent (*Jonah 3:10-4:2*). He could not stand to think of his own people not repenting and Nineveh repenting and being spared after Nineveh had done such harm and brought such suffering on the people of Israel. He had a heart problem that the Lord wanted to correct in him to prepare him for much greater ministry. God knew he would rebel. That's why He called him to that very task so He could bring Jonah to a point of blessing.

The dynamics of Jonah's case are interesting. It is interesting that Jonah knew without hesitation that it was God's Hand in the storm and that he was immediately willing to be thrown overboard to save the ship's crew (*Jonah 1:11-12*). Undoubtedly expecting to drown, he was eaten by a fish instead, and was left alive in the belly of the fish to ponder this new "affliction" (*Jonah 1:17*). This is where it gets interesting (a concept I did not realize until after my own experience discussed in the last chapter). Jonah's conclusion in his ponderings was to sacrifice to the Lord "with a voice of ***thanksgiving***!" (*Jonah 2:9*). It was then that the Lord delivered him from the belly of the fish and restored him to dry land (*Jonah 2:10*).

But that did not resolve the problem in Jonah's heart; it simply prepared him for the next level of affliction in God's wonderful plan for him. He went on to Nineveh and proclaimed the message. Chapter 3 is an amazing account of repentance of this huge city from the king down to every individual as a result of just one day of Jonah's preaching. Jonah was truly anointed by God, but Nineveh's repentance revealed Jonah's bitterness that the Lord would spare them. This set up the next affliction according to God's sovereign plan. Jonah would go out of the city to watch what would happen, angry that Nineveh would be spared (*Jonah 4:5*). As the Lord provided a vine to shade him and then took it away and afflicted him with a scorching heat (*Jonah 4:6-8*), God showed him His nature of compassion for the people of Nineveh "who do not know the difference between their right and left hand" (*Jonah 4:11*). What an enhancement this must have been to Jonah's on-going ministry as he learned of God's compassion amidst the Word of judgment and repentance he was called to speak.

Most things I feel strongly about have come to be part of my character and ministry through trial-like experiences (I spoke of some of these in the last chapter). God works new things in our lives through changes in our routine, through things that tend to disrupt our life, and through afflictions that are often very difficult to endure and move through with grace. Do we have to have enough *faith* to see God do these new things through these experiences? There are some things that are clear in His Word and that we are free to stand upon without doubt or debate from among our brethren in the Lord. One is that God is a good God who loves His children and always intends good things for them (*Rom 8:26-39*). He is an active God who brings about things in our lives that ultimately lead to wonderful and good things for us. We must rely on His judgment to determine what is good in each moment. We must approach our suffering with this knowledge in our minds, standing on the promises of His Word in these things regardless of the measure of faith we have been granted. This is the first thing that is needed. God will bring about the deeper faith in our hearts later, as we accept His work in the light of our understanding of His Word. (We will discuss "having faith" later).

◆ ◆ ◆

Questions for Meditation or Group Discussion

1. Think back on a time of hardship in your life that is now over (financial, physical, work struggles, marriage problems, damaged relationships, prolonged physical injury or disease...). How did that experience help to shape who you are now and how you respond to certain circumstances in a way that you might not have responded had you not gone through that hardship? How might that experience yet be working to shape your life in a positive way in building effective ministry? Looking back, do you believe that the hardship was a result of Satan's direct attack on you to prevent your coming closer to God, or do you feel it may have been God's plan all along that you experience that hardship? (Do you have a completely different explanation?)

2. Can you think of any Christians you know (or have known in the past) that used their hardship for great ministry to many people? What role do you feel God played in their afflictions if any?

3. Is it possible that God may allow significant hardship to come into our lives in order to build ministry within us and that ministry often does not happen because of the way we respond to the hardship? If so, what does this say

about the importance of God being absolutely sovereign in our lives?

4. When we speak of God disciplining us, what do you think that really means in terms of what God is ultimately trying to do?

5. Read the last few chapters of Job (*Job 38-42*). When we experience hardships of any kind, how important is it for us to know where the hardship came from or why we are experiencing it? Do you believe that God wants us to understand these things in order to experience the good that He promises in all things (*Rom 8:28*)? When the hardship is in the form of a physical affliction, is it reasonable to assume that the only *good* thing the Lord has in mind is physical healing? If we want all that God has for us in these experiences, what kind of response should we have to them while we are in them?

3

Using affliction to minister outside the Body of Christ

In chapter 2 we made two points (among others) about the suffering of a believer in general: 1) how we move through this suffering is what distinguishes us from the non-believer, and 2) God's purpose is to work wonderful, new, and fresh things in our lives through the suffering. These fresh things always lead to bringing the believer closer to the Heart of God in worship and ministry. With regard to the non-believer, the believer's suffering will tend to draw that person into the Light, primarily through the fact of point number 1 above. We *are* different, and the world sees it in times of trouble.

I think of a number of my friends at church whose suffering (unlike mine) brings horrendous physical disability, usually wheel chair-bound. But seeing their countenance in any situation when we are together brings a joy to the soul. It is impossible to feel pity or sorrow when with them because they radiate God's Presence. They are clearly in a place where those not yet in the Light could not possibly be or even fathom. Their anointing in the midst of their affliction is a huge encouragement to believers and a source of amazement to non-believers.

My friend Howard tells me of a very young man who was suddenly stricken with a terminal illness and bed-ridden for several months. This young man felt God's calling on him to use this time to intercede and pray for his friends and acquaintances for their salvation. As he prayed for them, one-by-one, these friends came to visit him in the hospital, and, there, he shared the Gospel with them. Over 250 people came to know the Lord in that hospital through this young man's calling before he died!

We are different from non-believers, and the world sees it and is drawn to where we are. There are a lot of good morally behaving people out there, but Christians are distinguished *by their response to affliction*. This is where significant ground is gained against the deceptions of the Enemy. The Spirit within us cannot be denied when His Grace is displayed in suffering.

My case is different from my friends above (as everyone's is different). I am terminally ill (with life expectancy measured in months) but I have no physical impairment or pain, I can communicate normally, and I continue to go to work everyday and am as productive as before (until the final couple of months when I'm told my health will decline quickly before death). I do not sense that I have a joyful countenance like others (a personality issue that I believe the Lord is addressing). But the Lord has granted me an intense desire to speak about my affliction and its effect on my life. And the Lord has placed me in an environment where this is particularly effective.

Several of my colleagues came to the house to visit immediately after my surgery. There I informed them (rather nonchalantly) of my terminal prognosis and when I was scheduled to die. Following their lead, I talked about my plans to "get my affairs in order" and how that was an important responsibility before God and before men (especially my family!). Then I quickly moved on to talk about my wonderful expectations within this situation because of what the Lord had been doing in my life, regardless of how things turned out. The group sat and listened very seriously and had no real response. Finally, one of them offered, "Well, one thing is for sure: when one sees a friend go through this, it certainly causes one to come face to face with one's own mortality." I then realized that the Lord had placed me in a very unique position for ministry.

Now, where I work, I am surrounded by intellectuals—mostly hard core secularists (college professors). They would normally not engage in spiritually-oriented conversation, and, if they did, it would be for the purpose of debating these "philosophical" issues. In my office, however, they don't debate. They can't because I am simply sharing my personal experience, and there is nothing to debate. They find themselves listening to me carry-on for 20 minutes while they come to grips with their own philosophy stacked up against their own mortality and realize how bankrupt their view is. I am always meeting colleagues in the coffee shop or in the halls who ask how I am "bearing up". "I'm dying but the Lord is really blessing me through the experience", I would generally say. Usually, they will show up at my office door a little later or, perhaps, the following day (remember, they want to talk about it!). They generally rise after a while (many times with tears in their eyes) and express that they have "a lot to think about". A colleague who had moved away returned to see me upon hearing of my condition. He was one of the few that had debated me in the past. I had had to confront him on some issues over creation-evolution as they touched on our work responsibilities. During one 2-hour discussion in his office, I had the opportunity to share the entire Gospel message with him (it was relevant to the business discussion!). He had expressed admiration for me back then that, as a scientist & engineer, I could put such faith in a book written 2,000 years ago that wasn't even "peer-reviewed by the editorial board of the Truth in Religion Journal" (or some such comment). Now he had returned to visit me and found himself (as many others had) sitting in my office listening to me carry on about the blessings of this affliction with nothing to say. When our visit was over, he had tears running down his face and said, "I wish I were where you are." I had the privilege of telling him how he could be there. Many colleagues and former students have come and sat with me to hear what I have to say. What a time of great blessing the Lord has brought at this stage of my life!

You see, this ministry was made possible and enabled because of this affliction. Because I learned to praise God while in the midst of the affliction, non-believers are drawn to it. The "death" aspect of my affliction has been a particularly powerful tool in my case, but I believe that the world is equally drawn to all believers when they respond to their particular affliction by reflecting God's Grace; and this response comes through praise and thanksgiving for that affliction because we trust in God's wonderful purposes in it. God brings the particular hardship to us that He has ordained for our appointed ministry—in the circumstances He has appointed for us, and for the people to whom He wants to minister through us. Let your reaction to and disposition about your affliction draw people to you; tell them what God is doing in your life as a result; let them see (from a believer's perspective) what it is like to have God's Grace in the midst of affliction; and gently lead them into the gospel message when they ask (or when it is clear that's what they want ask, but don't know how). Remember, this is what distinguishes those in the Light from those that are not! And affliction of the believer is the enabling foundation for that distinction. This is our motivation for praising Him and thanking Him for it.

◆ ◆ ◆

Questions for Meditation or Group Discussion

1. In this chapter, examples were provided of Christians who ministered to unbelievers through the circumstances of their affliction (the young man who led so many to Christ from his hospital bed, my opportunities to plant seeds among many in the midst of the death prognosis). Many believers with whom I have talked agree that they see this phenomena many times over within the Body, although usually not as dramatic and explicit as the hospital bed example. They talk of the general spirit, outlook, and conversation of these believers who are suffering and how this can only be attributed to the Holy Spirit. How many believers do you know (or have heard about) that you believe are displaying (or did display at the time) a behavior and overall spirit that you believe was from the Holy Spirit? Try to describe what you feel was in their hearts. How did these believers minister in ways unique to their personality and their particular affliction? How do you feel (or how did you feel) when you are in their presence? Does their behavior bring encouragement to you, and what does their behavior teach you about how we should respond and behave the next time we are hurting?

2. Do you know of any unbelievers who have gone through times of great suffering and seemed to have born it with dignity and with a good attitude and spirit? Were they an

example to others? How was their response different from the believers discussed above in the first question? More to the point, what kind of *ministry* was born from their suffering as opposed to the believers above?

3. Given these considerations, to what extent do you believe the Lord uses the afflictions of His children to draw unbelievers into the Light (compared to the many other ways He does so)? How important is a correct (obedient) response to our suffering to both our ministry to others and to our own spiritual growth in the Lord?

4

Using affliction to minister within the Body of Christ

How we respond to affliction as children of God provides a very distinct impression on the world that, I believe, is more powerful than any amount of preaching or direct sharing of the gospel in bringing the lost into the Light. But in my experience with affliction, the predominant impact has been in transforming my relationship with God and my ministry and in bringing encouragement to others within the Church.

In a way, the effect on believers of seeing our response to affliction is similar to the effect on non-believers. With believers, however, it is not something mysterious for which they have no knowledge. Therefore, it serves as an encouragement to take the next step in their growth that the Lord has laid before them. It is particularly encouraging to those currently experiencing hardship (and all of us experience hardship at one time or another).

Emphasizing the importance of intimate praise

When I share with fellow believers about my recent experiences (whether in times of casual fellowship or in times where someone hurting is seeking my counsel), I always simply tell my story (parts of it, as time allows), much as I have done here. But my story always comes to a bottom line that always speaks directly to their need. That bottom line nearly always includes the concept of thanking God for all of our hardships and entering into pure praise as a foundation for receiving what God has planned for us (*James 1:2-4*). I emphasize the nature of this "praise" as being pure adoration without distraction to other forms of worship and prayer that are important at other times of the day. As I stated earlier in the book, I believe this kind of pure praise is foundational to any effective ministry. However, I find that this does not speak very clearly to many believers. I can often see that it is received like a cliché as in "have faith" or "pray believing" or "have your quiet time every day".

On one occasion, I was addressing a group of about 50 believers in a fellowship organization at work, and I made this point about pure praise several times. During the question and answer period, someone asked a question that, at the time, seemed to come straight out of left field for me. He asked, "What do you mean by 'praising' God? What do you do practically? There is only so much time you can spend listening to praise music and thanking God for things." I immediately recognized that it was a very good and appropriate question. It was a question I might have asked just 3 years ago. But I struggled with the question on the floor, stumbled through a response, and, in the end, was very dissatisfied with my answer. I had clearly failed to communicate anything meaningful. I was faced with that same question at least twice over the next week from completely different people in different contexts. It was clear the Lord was challenging me to grow into a better position to articulate this meaningfully as an encouragement to believers. Two things consistently arose in my mind as central points:

1. The praise is personal between you and God. Therefore, it is not facilitated by the distraction of worship "enhancers" like praise music. I love praise music, and I have various electronic devices that I use to listen to praise music in various situations. But when I enter pure praise time before the Lord, I cannot depend on the praise words of a composer or the emotion-enhancing effect of well orchestrated musical sounds. I have to be totally exposed before the Lord with nothing inserted from outside. It is real praise when only God Himself places that praise in you as you lay yourself totally exposed before Him with your heart alone.

2. The primary characteristic of pure praise resides in the concept of ***intimacy*** with God. Depending on your church or particular fellowship background, you may have a good sense of this concept, but many believers do not. I think it is a particularly difficult concept for men. We

understand intimacy with our wives (even though our wives probably feel we still haven't fully grasped it), but it is difficult to envision by analogy that form of relationship with God, expressed intimately in a moment of praise. I really appreciate the Song of Solomon that describes so poetically the intimacy between a man and a woman. It is actually expressing the nature of how God wants to relate to *us*. It is a wonderful mystery for which the Lord gives us more and more understanding as we open ourselves to His moving in our hearts.

If you are reading this book and want to experience what I have been talking about, you deserve at least some practical expression of the things that I "do" when I enter into praise. In my case it has the following practical characteristics:

—I get completely alone in an undisturbed place that is well out of earshot of anyone in the house—everyone knows not to disturb me;

—in my mind, I lay all of my corrupt thoughts, motives, and emotions (including whether or not I'm "in the mood" for praise that day) at His feet and, then, leave them there, looking away from them and up toward Him;

—I remain on my feet, stretching out my hands with motions to express my feelings and speaking out loud boldly (I fall to the floor and bow before Him only when He prompts me to do so);

—I declare His sovereignty, His supreme authority, His mercy, and His grace;

—I ask for a mental and heart view of Him that is more worthy of Him; and

—I boldly declare my love for Him. I can never love Him like He loves me, and I know that, in this flesh, my love is always corrupt in many ways. But that is part of what is already laid at His feet. When I am in praise, I stand before Him and boldly declare (out loud), "I love you". I speak it continually until the barriers in my heart break down, and I finally know that I am expressing the real passion of my heart.

But these practical things do not express what is in my heart—I can't express that. Besides, I never understood it until God granted me the experience. I cannot prescribe a recipe for praise for others, and, ultimately, it is God that grants the experience and the heart-level understanding.

During my times of praise, there will generally come a time when I physically feel God's Presence around me (for me it is a warm tingling sensation), and I sense His smile and His pleasure in the praise. It is then that the praise is enhanced even more as God Himself blesses my heart with deeper praise for Him that seems to overflow until I am overcome with emotions I cannot express. This is joy like I have never experienced!

With the experience often comes something fresh—a sense of something the Lord wants to lead me into that day. It has never failed, in such cases, that circumstances arise that day that affirm this sense and begin to build another aspect of the foundation of ministry that is always under construction. It is usually also the case that my systematic Bible reading that day will miraculously speak to that very issue. For example, I remember early-on when I was just coming into understanding of the importance of praise, my worship one morning brought me to my knees, and I was swept up in the thought that only in this mind set and in this position before the Lord would anything of real substance come in ministry. Further, as such, it would be ministry not planned or even imagined by me but would be the work of the Father alone. As I tried to run that day (as I occasionally did just to confirm I was still afflicted with exercise intolerance), I remember thinking as I started out that I was already tired, and I fully expected that I would not even make my usual quarter mile. But I turned my thoughts to the Lord and entered into worship as I ran because my exhaustion reminded me that the Lord was working good things through these afflictions. As I became lost in worshipful thoughts, I ran 1.7 miles without stopping (the full length of the course I had laid out). I hadn't even realized I was running that far until I had finished. This was clearly miraculous—there is no way (even if I was healed of my condition) that I could have built up to that level in such short a time. But there was no building up—it was a sudden level of performance that was impossible without His miraculous intervention. And it didn't happen again in future attempts. He used the physical exercise performance that day to confirm the teaching He was bringing that day and to demonstrate how unexpected and even miraculous things happen in His Presence (through a mind and heart full of worship). And this lesson expanded even further. It was a joy to be able to share this as a miraculous intervention with people at work (I have been sharing my progress in disposition, fatigue, and strength with my co-workers). Sharing how the Lord used this in my life ministered to them and planted the lesson in my heart. That night regular Bible reading "miraculously" dealt with being in His Presence as the source of our strength and our delight. Strength comes from being in the Presence of the Lord and that strength is displayed within the world, flowing from the glow of His Presence that remains. This kind of daily experience (in worship and in growing into new ministry understanding and experience) is a foundational part of a growing Christian's life, and it comes from knowing *intimacy* with God.

Within the Body of Christ, it appears this intimacy is "seen" in those continually experiencing it. I've talked earlier about other believers sensing God's presence on me (even though I feel the same as I have for years). After speaking one day at a fellowship group, an older brother in the Lord approached me to apologize if he seemed distracted during my talk (I hadn't noticed). He explained that God's Presence was so strong that he was compelled to close his eyes and worship. He looked me straight in the eye and told me in a very affirming tone, "You've sat in the Presence of God." You and I know that I don't deserve the privilege of being seen that way, and I am awed by the thought. But I believe it is an anointing of the Spirit that every Christian is intended to have as we fellowship together. It is the primary ingredient of real fellowship and real growth in the Body.

Back to subject of this book, I came in to these experiences and blessings when I thanked God and praised Him for my afflictions. The Lord promises affliction in the world (*John 16:33*), and I wonder if He has ordained affliction as the pathway to intimacy with Him from which He can effect all of His wonderful purposes in us. In the midst of your affliction, let other believers see and experience the fresh anointing of the Spirit emanating from one who "has sat in the Presence of God"—(<u>intimacy is the key</u>). This has been the primary ministry within the Body of Christ that I have seen God perform in my case. But there are other areas of ministry that have arisen.

Ministering to those in affliction

When other believers see God's grace on us in the midst of hardship, they are encouraged and, hopefully, learn not to fear affliction when it comes. But for those in the midst of serious physical and emotional affliction, special ministry is needed. It is not sufficient to be an example and encourage them to "come around". These afflictions are debilitating as the Enemy uses them to deceive and distract and to destroy one's joy in the Lord. Ultimately, it is the Lord who delivers from discouragement, but He uses the Body of Christ to do this good work.

We are surely called to minister encouragement to the brethren in this area and to give them full benefit of our experience in the Lord. Brethren will continually ask ever present questions (what about those with very physically debilitating diseases, what about those who die and are not healed; what about their families left behind; etc.). It's really always the same answer with lots of opportunity to couch it in terms relevant to the specific question. We must learn to rejoice and give thanks in our afflictions and give God the praise He is due. Here are some questions for believers who are suffering—to lead them to the intended blessing:

—**Do you love God and believe that He loves you?**

—**Do you believe He is in sovereign control of our circumstances?**

—**Do you believe His Word when He says that He works all things together for our good and for His glory?** *(Rom 8:28)*

(Most Christians will respond "yes" to these questions because they know that it is the "right" answer and because they really want to believe these things in their hearts and minds. <u>*That is all that is needed*</u>. Move on to the next question. God is not waiting for them to straighten things out, or get their hearts right, or conjure up enough "faith" to make it happen. <u>*He provides that after the fact*</u>! This is a significant and amazing blessing discussed further below.

> **—Do you believe He wants us to learn to ask Him for these blessings that are "for our good and for His glory"?**
>
> **—Do you believe His Word when He says that He inhabits the praise of His people?** *(Psalm 22:3)*
>
> (His Presence amidst our praise *is* the foundational blessing. It trumps any lack of understanding we have concerning how to appropriate God's full intent in our afflictions. If He is dwelling in our praise, then that is blessing enough; and all of His intended blessings will flow from that alone.)

From this position, the believer simply needs to step forward in every ministry opportunity God provides in each moment. We can release our intellect and our reasoning on how to properly orchestrate receiving His blessings. He will provide everything in His time and in His way. Only He knows the full richness of what He has planned.

If we teach these simple things within the Body as we demonstrate an example of God's grace in our own hardship, then we are obedient in fellowship and encouragement to our brethren. Just as we can't orchestrate how the Lord blesses us, so we can't orchestrate how the Lord brings others to that point. We can ponder how different believers may be coming from different contextual backgrounds, and we can strategize how to "reason" with them to bring them to a point we think will move them into the Lord's blessings, but I regard this as rather arrogant. Are there, in fact, prerequisites that we must help others achieve before the Lord provides His blessings (being in proper fellowship with a supporting Body of Believers, a right baseline view of God Himself, an openness to the possibility of God desiring and intending intimate worship, faith that God intends good things in the affliction, etc.)? These are the kinds of issues that might be discussed for perspective, but <u>they are solved in God's Presence</u>! I feel I need to emphasize this point. To present guidelines for leading someone to a place where they are ready for intimate worship may imply that there are works-based prerequisites that do not exist. God may lead His children through stages of development, but it is not our place to design and orchestrate this on behalf of a specific person in a specific circumstance and a specific place spiritually. Be an example of God's grace in affliction (let God show Himself in you through your intimate worship), point the brother or sister to intimate thanksgiving and praise with the five simple bold-faced questions above, and, while praying for them, let God draw them in to a new and wonderful experience.

The question of "faith"

Another dominant area of ministry displayed in my case is that of reassuring those in the midst of hardship that their plight is not necessarily a disciplining of their misbehavior and certainly not a punishment for their "lack of faith" (it certainly wasn't in Job's case). This thinking reflects a very serious attack of the Enemy that <u>must be confronted</u>.

I am very familiar with words that instruct us to pray in faith for healing and believe that God will do so. It is common language among most of those with whom I fellowship. But the words took on a new character when they were applied to *my* affliction. I was appalled when a trusted sister counseled my wife to have faith and believe that God was healing my terminal cancer—to "stand on the Word" for promise of long life. You see, I had a different perspective on my affliction. I was focused on God's blessing and ministry being performed in the affliction, not on believing in healing. I had entered a new area of ministry that was expanding every day, without any regard for whether or not I would be physically healed. Moreover, I was aware of many others in the Lord who had ministered in tremendous ways in their illnesses and several who had gone on into the full Presence of the Lord in such a way that many came to know the Lord through witnessing the manner in which they died (for example, the young man in the hospital that I spoke of in chapter 3). I'm ready for that. I understand the good intentions (and the specific perspective) of the counsel being given to my wife. But I suddenly realized what incredible destruction this counsel would cause should my calling include ministering through my death in the near future. How would Sherry go on in the wake of my death wondering if I was gone because *she* did not have the faith to prevent it? It occurred to me that those giving such counsel would be very wise to consider whether such counsel is correct. (This is not to say that I don't pray for healing and desire a long life of ministry. But I yield to His higher purposes in His sovereign Will in such prayers.)

After speaking at many places and many forums about my experience, I approached one of our associate pastors about speaking at our church (I had had no such opportunity at that point in time except in my Sunday School class and in fellowship with many people individually). Our church is medium in size (about 2,000 attending) with a large ministry staff, so there is a protocol for these kinds of things. I had a 3 p.m. appointment on Wednesday afternoon to tell this pastor my story and to recount the many blessings the Lord had provided through it. After about 45 minutes, he decided to give me the entire Wednesday service that night (3 hours warning!). He had just begun teaching the Book of James the previous week and had focused on the exhortation to

> **consider it all joy, my brethren, when you encounter various trials, knowing that the testing of your faith produces endurance. And let endurance have its perfect result, so that you may be perfect and complete, lacking in nothing.**
>
> *(James 1:2-4, NAS)*

The pastor felt that I would be the perfect example from within our own Body to come and talk about the experience of putting that into practice. The whole situation seemed to be God-appointed. I spoke for 45 minutes, emphasizing at the end the correct response to affliction. I talked about taking authority over the Enemy (as mentioned in chapter 21) but focused on the response of thanksgiving and praise in the midst of the affliction and the bounty of blessings that would ensue.

At the end, the pastor called for people to come forward who needed to be released from their fears and struggles with their hardships. *Half the congregation responded.* I had the privilege of praying over them for release from fear and doubt concerning the reason for their affliction or their faith to overcome it. I led them in a prayer of praise <u>for</u> their afflictions, and there was a marvelous outpouring of the Spirit. Several people spoke to me afterwards declaring how much they had struggled with the issue of having faith for healing and the release they now felt. They now finally realized that it is God who gives faith and that our command is to rejoice in all things until such time as we have discernment on how to pray and fully realize God's purposes in the affliction. Several approached me in the weeks that followed to share with me that that night had completely changed their prayer life. It is clear that many believers are hungry for this message and that the Lord wants to do something new and fresh for all of us in the midst of our hardships.

◆ ◆ ◆

Questions for Meditation or Group Discussion

1. Many (like myself who has spent years teaching the Bible) can say that we have "grown the Word", that is, we have grown in knowledge of the Bible which has, in many ways, imparted wisdom to our hearts. But had I been challenged (as I eventually challenged myself) to give an account of my growth in *ministry* within the Body, I would have had very little to show that I was aware of. When I learned the concept of becoming intimate with God and knowing (in a real, tangible way) His daily *Presence* in my life, I saw and bore witness to the ministry that the Lord performed through me that could not be attributed to my planning or my particular preparation (that is, *real ministry*). Relate this to your own experience. Describe the nature of your ministry within the Body of Christ and the fruit you have seen born. How clearly do you see God's Hand in the fruit? How were these times related to your personal praise before the Lord? How, in your opinion, is real fruit in ministry related to your praise of God on a daily basis and the intensity of that praise?

2. Do you know people within the Body who seem to have an *air* about them, who seem to emanate a *presence* about them that you attribute to the Holy Spirit or to their *closeness* to the Lord? Do you believe that this is a special anointing of the Lord for that person and a few chosen

others, or do you believe (or wonder) that this is intended for all believers? We can all claim the clear promise that we have received the Holy Spirit (*Eph 1:13-14*), but do you feel that others can *see* that fact in you? If not, and if the Lord wants that for you, how does it happen? Do you have any role in it, or does God just choose *if* and *when* according to His sovereign plan?

3. To what extent have you come to value (really hunger after) the Presence of God in your life? Have you come to the point that, regardless of the degree of hardship or affliction in your life, the knowledge and experience of His Presence with you is blessing enough, no matter how the hardship plays out?

4. The question of having enough faith is a big issue in the Body of Christ. The words are often spoken without a crystal clear reference as to what it is we are to have faith *in* within the particular circumstance. In your opinion, what is faith, how do you come to have faith, and to what extent must we have it in order to experience the blessings God intends for each of us to have?

5

A word on "healing"—the different views

In previous chapters, I have alluded to different approaches within the Body of Christ in responding to affliction (most clearly demonstrated in the talk with my chaplain friend concerning his struggle within his congregations over *claiming healing* in all cases of sickness). Within affliction, many would teach that we should concentrate on a promise of healing; whereas I and many others would teach that we should focus on God's full purpose in the affliction which is appropriated through praise amidst the affliction. This is a significant issue that really must be dealt with in this book to be complete. As I start writing this chapter, I sense it will be the most difficult to write and much of it will go counter to the views of many of my dear friends in the Lord. Therefore, I must ask for grace from the reader as I attempt a difficult subject, asking the Lord to guide my thoughts.

I am familiar with most of the scriptures speaking to healing of God's children, and I have tried to reconcile them with my personal experience in the Lord. I find that it is quite easy to do so, and I am confident that the Lord is blessing the message I am speaking. Of course, there are many aspects of affliction and many kinds of affliction. There are also differences in where we each are in the Lord and what the Lord is doing in our lives. And we must never lose sight of the fact that we are in a spiritual battle in which we dare not give any ground to the Enemy when the Lord is calling us to battle. Therefore, I encourage the reader to consider what I have to say and receive it in light of my experience (understanding that I love the Lord and believe in His infallible Word and that we must stand on the clear promises of His Word). Then see how the Lord directs you amidst your own experiences in hardship and affliction and your own understanding and discernment of His Word.

I am often confronted with this issue when speaking with believers about my experience. One of the interesting things about interacting with individuals in the Body is the "other common reaction" to my condition. Many whose walk with the Lord and whose ministering spirit I trust, upon hearing of my affliction and hearing me talk about it, will immediately say something to the effect that they are "not receiving it" or they "rebuke it" or they are "believing right now that I am healed in the Name of Jesus". I usually say something like "Yes, Praise God", because I want to acknowledge their encouragement and exhortation. And, it would be nice to be in full agreement with them, but I always have a deep sense that they are just not getting it. It's interesting how they can stand there and rebuke the affliction while I'm standing there praising God for it! There is something that just isn't coming together right within the Body of Christ on this issue.

Let's look, for the moment, at a couple of scriptures that demonstrate this tension:

> **Because he has loved Me, therefore I will deliver him; I will set him securely on high because he has known My name.**
> **He will call upon Me, and I will answer him;**
> **I will be with him in trouble;**
> **I will rescue him and honor him.**
> **With a long life I will satisfy him**
> **And let him see My salvation.**
>
> *(Psalm 91: 14-16, NAS)*

> **Bless the Lord, O my soul,**
> **And forget none of His benefits;**
> **Who pardons all your iniquities,**
> **Who heals all your diseases;**
> **Who redeems your life from the pit,**
> **Who crowns you with loving-kindness and compassion;**
> **Who satisfies your years with good things,**
> **So that your youth is renewed like the eagle.**
>
> *(Psalm 103: 2-5, NAS)*

(Teth)
Before I was afflicted I went astray,
But now I keep your word.
You are good and do good;
Teach me your statutes...
It is good for me that I was afflicted,
That I may learn Your statutes.
The law of your mouth is better to me
Than thousands of gold and silver pieces.
(Yodh)
Your hands made and fashioned me;
Give me understanding, that I may learn Your commandments.
May those who fear You see me and be glad,
Because I wait for Your word.
I know, O Lord, that your judgments are righteous,
And that in faithfulness You have afflicted me.

(Psalm 119: 67-68, 71-75, NAS)

The first two passages are wonderful psalms of praise speaking to God's awesome love and mercy to us. It is very easy (particularly amidst affliction) to delight in these verses and say,

> "This is for me! I am *promised* that He will heal all my physical diseases and give me long life and restore my health like I was when I was young! All I have to do is '*claim*' the promise and '*believe*' it!"

Now, not all of my friends who lean toward this way of thinking would say this (although some do), and I don't mean to belittle their position. These friends are deep in the Word, and I trust their walk with the Lord. But, you see, I identify more with the third scripture above. I see so many of my brothers and sisters in the Lord (those who *fear* Him) express gladness when they see me because of what the Lord is doing in me within the affliction. I have learned His "statutes" in the midst of it (the deeper nature of His Presence, the blessings of intimate praise, His pleasure and grace and blessing when we thank him in our various trials, the manner in which he uses these things to bring ministry to believers and draw nonbelievers to Him…). Within this experience, I simply have not sought out scripture references that I might cling to as promises of healing. Why would I? The Lord's sovereign hand is clearly working His Will in the experience, and I don't need any "promises" to know that He will continue to do that as I continue to praise Him in the midst of my trials. Besides, when this one is over, there will be another one on its heels with even richer blessings in store from the Lord.

I mentioned earlier that I had spoken at the Gospel Service on a military base at the invitation of my chaplain friend. It was a wonderful time for me in that I felt the Lord's anointing in the words and the response. Among the many who hugged me after the service, a young man talked with me and said, "I now see and understand for the first time that God uses these afflictions for growing and preparing us for ministry; how then can we refuse them and rebuke them?" I just feel that we are often too quick to assume that we have a right to be pain-free and hardship-free as God's children, when I'm not sure we've really been promised that. In fact, Jesus seems to promise quite the opposite. **"In the world you shall have tribulation: but be of good cheer; I have overcome the world."** (*John 16:33b*). The most visible and tangible affliction we encounter is physical disease, and, therefore, it receives a lot of attention in teaching. There seems to be a strong teaching within the Body that physical disease is not among the afflictions we are promised or to which we are vulnerable as children of God. This teaching further says that we should be speaking against such afflictions to gain victory over them in accordance with the "promises" of the Word. (I praise God that this was not my response to my disease. Perhaps, standing some day before His throne, I will learn of the even greater blessings He had in store for me had I responded that way, but I don't think so.)

Claiming our healing for our own sake (that is, as a promise of God to us) seems off the mark in light of the purpose of healing. When Jesus was asked about the man born blind (that is, was it he or his parents who sinned), Jesus replied, **"It was neither that this man sinned, nor his parents; but it was so that the works of God might be displayed in him."** (*John 9:3, NAS*). Jesus then healed the man, and glory was brought to God in the man's testimony. The point is always how God will bring glory to Himself, and that is what we must focus our hearts and minds toward. Our healing in and of itself is never the point and should not be the focus of our desire and expectation.

One of the problems with claiming promises in the Word is knowing whether or not the passage is really speaking a promise. Very seldom do we see (in English) the word *promise* in the scriptures. When God spoke to Abraham, Jacob, Moses, and David He established a "covenant" with His people which I take to be a contract or a "promise" that God will always fulfill from His end. Looking for promises beyond this, particularly in the area of healing, may be inappropriate in seeking and applying God's Word. What we know is that God's Word is true, and He blesses our understanding of the *Truth* as we seek His Word, praying for understanding and wisdom. There are some things in the Word that are generally and universally clear. For example, **"I am the way, and the truth, and the life; no one comes to the Father but through Me"** (*John 14:6, NAS*). **"...there is no other Name under heaven that has been given among men by which we must be saved"** (*Acts 4:12, NAS*). **"...you were sealed in Him with the Holy Spirit of promise, who is given as a pledge of our inheritance."** (*Ephesians 1:13-14, NAS*). Or, **"we know that God causes all things to work together for good to those who love God, to those who are called according to His purpose"** (*Rom 8:28, NAS*). Praise God for this glorious truth! We can stand on these truths with boldness and confidence. The issue of physical healing, however, is far less clear to me.

I find that there are a lot of verses that reference healing, but very few passages (none, that I have found) whose purpose is to teach on the subject of physical healing. This is a case where we need to be very careful about what we teach. The passage that comes closest to expressly talking about physical healing is in James:

> **Is anyone among you suffering? Then he must pray. Is anyone cheerful? He is to sing praises. Is anyone among you sick? Then he must call for the elders of the church and they are to pray over him, anointing him with oil in the name of the Lord; and the prayer offered in faith will restore the one who is sick, and the Lord will raise him up, and if he has committed sins, they will be forgiven him. Therefore, confess your sins to one another, and pray for one another so that you may be healed. The effective prayer of a righteous man can accomplish much.**
>
> *(James 5: 13-16, NAS)*

This is one of several specific exhortations given to the church in James 5. I believe it is talking about physical illness, and we are to gather the elders to pray over the sick. It is also clear that a prayer of *faith* will "restore" the sick. (The exhortation is linked to the concept of confessing sins to one another as a life-style practice in the Body so that we may be healed—clearly a topic worthy of expanded teaching). Now, I don't see that this passage provides any promise that <u>all</u> in the Body who are sick are to be healed, as if to say that we must "have faith" that God will heal anyone who is sick, and, then, He will do it. If this passage teaches that all are to be healed, then why doesn't it clearly say so? And why do we not see such a teaching corroborated elsewhere in the scripture? (Of course, many would say that it *is*, which is why there is tension within the Body on this point).

I consider the case of Paul who declared that he was given a "thorn in the flesh" and refers to it as an "infirmity" (2 *Corinthians 12:7-10)*. Paul never explicitly declares what the infirmity is, but it seems clear in context that it is some kind of physical affliction. Paul asks the Lord three times to be delivered (I believe in the same sense that I often ask for healing of my cancer). Not only does the Lord not deliver him, but Paul speaks of "glorying" and "taking pleasure" in his infirmities in this passage. Furthermore, in 1 Timothy 5, Paul does not rebuke Timothy for not having faith and not claiming healing of his "frequent" infirmities. Instead he recommends medication. ***"Drink no longer water, but use a little wine for your stomach's sake and your frequent infirmities". (1 Tim 5:23)***. (When I was in college, this is exactly what the doctor prescribed for my stomach problems!). These cases were, apparently, cases that did not call for a measure of faith to overcome, but were being used of God for good purposes (God explicitly told Paul this in the Corinthians passage). So, if the prayer offered in faith will restore the one who is sick, then we must understand what it means to "pray in faith".

When I have talked with believers who appear to have the gift of healing (as repeatedly demonstrated by seemingly miraculous healing or deliverance in response to their prayers), there seem to be two conditions that apply to such incidents. Either they discern a specific unholy spirit mounting an attack against the person and they respond by taking authority over it, or they discern (as part of their gift) God's desire to bring physical healing as the blessing He intends in that particular case. Having that discernment, they pray with the *faith* that simply comes with knowing God's Will in that moment. I have never met anyone who always sees miraculous healing when they respond in obedience to praying for the sick. Many over whom they pray are not healed, and they never receive any sense from the Lord that physical healing was intended in those cases. Were those cases examples of a *lack of faith*?

In my early years, I was in a church environment where the phrase "pray in faith" was big. It seemed to be the bottom line of over half the Sunday School lessons taught. Everyone knew the words and often used them to encourage people going through hard times. As I look back on it now, I see a culture of words that had very little real impact in peoples' lives. I saw no miraculous deliverances or great revivals or strong movements of the Holy Spirit. I remember one time in Sunday School I asked, "What do we mean by 'praying in faith'? How does one do that?" It became one of the more interesting classes I experienced in those days. After the initial knee-jerk responses of "well, it means to believe God will answer your prayer" (which isn't responsive to the question), we became stalemated, with someone pointing out that God always answers prayer by saying "yes", "no", or "wait", which, of course, no one could argue with; but the real issue was left unresolved. How can we "believe" that God will *grant* (say "yes" to) our prayers when we don't know if the request is in His perfect will for us to pray? We must either *know* it clearly from His Word or sense or discern His Will in the situation through an intimate fellowship with Him, such that we know His heart and mind in the circumstances. This is the characteristic of the righteous man in James chapter 5—one who is in the Presence of God and knows God's heart in that circumstance. In circumstances where the Lord intends healing, this man calls for God's healing with a "prayer of faith" and prays an "effective" prayer that will "accomplish much"; that is, it represents God's Will, and it will yield much blessing beyond the granting of the request itself. This man is intimate with God. (Intimacy with God was *not* a big thing in the churches where I grew up).

We cannot conjure up faith in every situation where we want God to move in a certain way. I just don't believe we have that power. God grants the faith as He reveals His Will within the circumstances. It is then revealed to us how we need to pray to fulfill that Will. We can *act* like we have faith by speaking in confident tones that something is "already done" when there is no outward evidence of such. But I don't think God needs that kind of "help" from us in answering our prayers after we have prayed. I remember a friend who was at our house for a social who had continuing struggles with migraine headaches. She had recently been taught to "pray in faith" by speaking correctly after praying for healing. She was afflicted with the start of a migraine while at the social. She prayed and claimed God's healing over the affliction. She then carried on and declared to everyone that her headache was gone. She continued to declare this anytime someone would ask how she felt until, finally, she was forced to retreat to a back bedroom to lie down with a cold cloth and complete darkness to suffer through the migraine episode (which had never really subsided).

My pastor cautions us to avoid what he calls "symptom semantics". So many believers will pray for healing and then guard their language in order to preserve an "attitude of faith". For example, they might encourage one of my friends who has been diagnosed with ALS (Lou Gehrig's disease) not to say that he *has* ALS (even though he shows all the symptoms and is wheel-chair bound); rather, he should say that he has the *symptoms* of ALS, as if God would refuse to heal him if he slipped up and actually said he had the disease after he had prayed for healing. I believe that if my friend ever actually spoke that way in contradiction to what was clearly evident, it would diminish God's power and sovereignty in his life. God does not demand magical phrases or words or actions to preserve His Will. He wants believers who are intimate with Him and know His Will and pray accordingly. Then they will see His immediate response in bringing about His revealed intentions without having to pretend something that isn't true.

Well, this brings us back to the question of whether or not we can have faith for physical healing based on God's written Word. Does the Word teach that it is God's desire and intent to bring healing in every case of physical affliction on any of His children? Can we (on that basis) pray in faith to see that healing realized? Again, I have great difficulty seeing any passage that directly teaches on that subject. I feel that the scriptures that are used to make that point are isolated verses that reference healing amidst a larger passage that is dealing with something completely different; that these scriptures are largely taken out of context. There is a preponderance of such scripture (healing is a common scriptural concept), and it appears to me that the mere volume of reference to healing is what is being used to make the case. A common and very familiar passage used in this regard is in Isaiah 53.

> **But He was pierced through for our transgressions,**
> **He was crushed for our iniquities;**
> **The chastening for our well-being fell upon Him,**
> **And by His scourging we are healed.**
> **All of us like sheep have gone astray,**
> **Each of us has turned to his own way;**
> **But the Lord has caused the iniquity of us all**
> **To fall on Him.**
>
> *(Isaiah 53:5-6, NAS)*

By His scourging we are healed or "by His stripes we are healed", as the KJV puts it, referring to His suffering and shedding of His Blood for our sins. There are many, many dimensions of healing that we require. Clearly the most critical of these is our sin nature that cuts us off from fellowship with the Lord and that condemns us to death with no hope within ourselves to remedy. The entire 53rd chapter of Isaiah is, perhaps, the best known prophecy of the coming Messiah who will take all our iniquities onto Himself and make the necessary atonement—restoring our fellowship with Him and *healing* this hopeless affliction of sin. This passage (with the specific reference to the shedding of His Blood) is not talking about physical healing of the child of God; it is talking about our healing from sin that allows us to *become* children of God. The context of this verse within this Messianic passage makes this clear.

I realize that Isaiah 53 is a cornerstone passage for many who believe that it declares our physical healing is already accomplished (and therefore merely needs to be claimed in faith). Several have encouraged me to consider the passage in the original language, which I take to mean that I should consider the Hebrew word that is rendered "healed" in the English. The word is *raphah*, which is just as ambiguous in the Hebrew language as the word "heal" is in English. Clarity is achieved and ambiguity removed when the word is considered in context. Again, the context of this Messianic passage makes it clear that Isaiah 53:5 is referring to our spiritual healing from sin. This is further affirmed by God's Word in 1 Peter, where Peter makes it clear this is the proper interpretation of this Isaiah passage which he specifically makes reference to:

> **For you have been called for this purpose, since Christ also suffered for you, leaving you an example for you to follow in His steps, who committed no sin, nor was any deceit found in His mouth; and while being reviled, He did not revile in return; while suffering, He uttered no threats, but kept entrusting Himself to Him who judges righteously; and He Himself bore our sins in His body on the cross, so that we might die to sin**

and live to righteousness; for by His wounds you were healed. For you were continually straying like sheep, but now you have returned to the Shepherd and Guardian of your souls.

(1 Pet 2:21-25, NAS)

There are many other verses that do speak of literal physical healing (I believe), but do they provide the promise we are looking for? Let me present seven representative passages that are often used to encourage us to have faith in healing along with my personal thoughts on their significance (i.e. what I would say if I were asked to teach on these passages). (Quotes are from the KJV)

<u>**Exodus 15:26**</u> **If you will diligently hearken to the voice of the Lord your God, and will do that which is right in His sight, and will give ear to His commandments, and keep all His statutes, I will put none of these diseases upon you, which I have brought upon the Egyptians: for I *am* the Lord that heals you.**

> Context: The history of the people of Israel is a type of or analogy to God's plan for us as we are redeemed (brought out of Egypt) and as we struggle in this corrupt world to know God more and more and be transformed into His likeness (the struggles of the wanderings and the search for peace in the prom-

ised land). This passage is speaking of God's delivering from Pharaoh and providing in the wilderness. It is a promise that if they obey, He will put none of the Egyptian diseases on them.

Significance for me: The teaching I perceive for my life is that I have been delivered from destruction eternally; I have crossed the Red Sea and will never again be subject to the fate of the unredeemed because I have obeyed the call to receive Jesus' Blood for my atonement. It is the Lord who provides this healing.

Exodus 23: 2 4-2 6 **You shall not worship their gods, nor serve them, nor do according to their deeds; but you shall utterly overthrow them and break their sacred pillars in pieces. And you shall serve the Lord your God, and He shall bless your bread, and your water; and I will take sickness away from the midst of you. There shall nothing cast their young, nor be barren, in your land: the number of your days I will fulfill.**

Context: Promises concerning conquest of the land. All enemies will be driven out (little by little) until they inherit the land. None are to remain and all their images cast down. Serve the Lord and He will provide.

Significance for me: For the Israelites, this was a clear promise that if they completely separated themselves from the ways of their enemies and utterly defeated them in God's power (little by little), he would lead them into good health and prosperity. He did, in fact, bless their bread and water and provide a healthy lifestyle through many of the laws provided in Leviticus. For me, I am delivered, and an abundant life of driving Satan out of every area of my life (little by little) will enable the Lord to give further victory. He will provide "bread" and "water" and "take sickness away". This is associated with obedience and total victory in areas of our lives. I take "bread" and "water" to refer to the tools of victory—the anointing with gifts of ministry that sweep away obstacles (sickness) that would thwart that ministry. In some cases, those obstacles might be physical disease (hence, gifts of ministry in healing). In my case, my physical sickness has enhanced my ministry.

Proverbs 10:27 **The fear of the Lord prolongs life, But the years of the wicked will be shortened.**

Significance for me: This verse speaks of the effect of the "fear of the Lord" in bringing "long life". This is a cause-effect statement, not a promise. If I want to be healed because I am dwelling on the affliction, if I believe that I am supposed to somehow conquer the affliction by claiming promises, and if it is not happening, I can't conjure up a "fear of the Lord" in order to claim a "promise" of long life. I must experience the fear of the Lord in what He is doing today in my life, without regard for His intention in physical healing. When my desires about physical healing are swept away by His Presence in the midst of the affliction, then the whole issue of physical healing is a non-issue. If I then experience long life, I can look back on this verse and declare its truth. But I can't manipulate God's plan and His work in my life by trying to conjure up something in my heart in order to be healed in the way I want.

Matthew 4: 2 3-2 4; Matthew 8: 16; Matthew 9:35; Matthew 12: 15; Mark 6: 5 5-5 6; Luke 4: 3 9-4 0; Luke 6: 1 7-1 9

Context: Matthew 4 is breezing through an account of Jesus' temptation, His move to Capernaum in Galilee, and the beginning of His ministry of preaching. They brought all manner of sick and possessed people to Him and "**He healed them**". Matthew 8 & Luke 4 recount the events after Jesus heals Peter's mother-in-law. They brought many who were possessed. He released them with a word and healed **all** who were sick. Matthew 8:17 explicitly says this was done to fulfill prophecy. Matthew 9 is a long passage focusing on Jesus' ministry of healing. Everyone who came to Him was apparently healed. Matthew 12 (as in Luke 6) says, **"Many followed and He <u>healed them all</u>."** In Mark 6 the people brought the sick to him in throngs. They asked to touch the hem of his garment, and all who did were healed.

Significance for me: It is not clear who these people were that were healed or whether or not they became believers. Therefore, it is difficult to conclude how this relates to a promise of healing for all believers. The argument is generally presented that we are to emulate Jesus in every way. That is, since Jesus healed all who were brought to him, then all whom we pray for should be healed. It is difficult for me to take the concept of being like Jesus to this extreme. Jesus was fulfilling prophecy in all that He did, and His healing ministry authenticated His message and pointed to His ultimate work. I want to be like Jesus in knowing the heart and mind of the Father and following in obedience. This is not achieved by assuming I will do exactly as He was called to do. I believe these passages are an account of Jesus' actions, not a direct teaching on healing.

Mark 11: 24

"Therefore I say to you, all things for which you pray and ask, believe that you have received them, and they will be granted you." *(NAS)*

Context: Jesus had cursed a fig tree, it had withered, and the disciples took note. Jesus then taught that whatever they prayed, believing it had been granted, without doubting, they would receive.

Significance for me: This is always the sticking point. You can't pray a "believing" prayer without knowledge that you are in God's Will (either by standing on the clear Word or by direct discernment). Discernment comes within the specific incident, and I have yet to see anywhere in the Word that all believers are to be healed of physical disease in every instance.

Mark 16: 18

Context: Just before ascending, Jesus declares what signs will accompany <u>believers</u>; among them, **"they will lay hands on the sick and they will recover"**.

Significance for me: I believe that this is, indeed, a sign among believers. But if I lay hands on someone and they don't recover, am I not a believer? I assume it must be accompanied by "believing" prayer, which means we must know God's Will in the situation. Is it God's Will for <u>all</u> to be healed upon whom believers lay their hands? I can't find this in the Word.

John 14: 14 — **Whatever you ask <u>in My Name</u>, I will do it.**

Significance for me: This is the ultimate point that bears on the entire discussion. "In My Name" means by His authority which means we are asking according to His wishes which means we are in intimate fellowship with Him, knowing His Will and believing!! This passage is certainly not giving us free reign to declare things we think are right by simply speaking the magic formula, "In Jesus' Name."

My purpose is not to argue or debate the scriptures. I am not qualified to do that. I am qualified to speak to what the Lord has done in my life through my affliction when I rejoiced in it and claimed the promise of His working it for good. In reviewing scripture, I cannot find that I have been disobedient or lacking in faith by not having declared healing from this disease. In my case, the Enemy has been unable to use this affliction against me because He could find no place amidst my praise and thanksgiving.

Don't get me wrong. I'm not sitting around waiting for death under some assumption that God has appointed me to death. I have gone to the elders for prayer as we are instructed to do. My wife anoints me every night and prays for my healing (because she is obedient to the Word and because this is the desire of our heart). I continually ask God to allow me to see <u>more ministry</u> being built in me. And He has given my wife and me a sense that He is preparing us for long term ministry (not short term). In the meantime, I continue to praise God for what He is doing within my affliction, and I continue to see His fresh blessing on a daily basis.

I have also been prayed over by a pastor who has had a very large church grow up around his prayer ministry. A good friend brought me to him for prayer, and the pastor declared that I would not die, that I would see my grandchildren (he wouldn't have known I hadn't seen them yet), and that I would become a great preacher! (I have been doing a lot of preaching since then!)

These things are encouraging to us, and we have great expectations that the Lord will bring healing. We continue to pray for my healing, and we accept the prayers of others on my behalf. **But I have never declared my healing in Jesus' Name.** The Spirit has not given me that to pray. I have no direct discernment concerning my healing, and I see no basis in the scripture to claim it. This is confirmed in my case by the blessing flowing from these circumstances. What I can pray for confidently is for Him to continue to bring to perfection everything He has started to build in me <u>through</u> the affliction. *That* I can stand on in the Word (*Phil 1:6*), and, in *that*, I can rejoice and praise God in obedience and in thanksgiving. Must we stand against the Enemy and declare his work void when he oppresses us with physical affliction? You bet! But I sense no evil presence whatsoever in this affliction. I only see the moving of God's Hand.

We all need discernment in each of our circumstances concerning what the Lord wants to do. He wants us to pray according to His Will in each case. That knowledge comes when we know His heart through an intimate fellowship with Him. I have learned that this comes when we praise and adore Him in the midst of our afflictions. If we are to rebuke the Enemy and defeat his attack, the Lord will tell us. If we are to be healed as a sign to believers and unbelievers upon our prayer of faith for healing, He will tell us. If we are to remain afflicted as a tool for ministry, He will pour out His fruitful blessings amidst the affliction when we continue to praise him for it. If we are to be afflicted in order to learn better how to approach Him intimately, then I am ready for this affliction and the next. If, in His Sovereign Grace, He does not reveal the purpose of the affliction, then I will praise and adore Him for the good purposes I know He must be working, because I stand on His Word on that point (*Rom 8:28*).

In such cases, it is not a lack of faith or an obstinate rebellion to declare that these things are not clear. **It's OK to say we don't understand. The key in these cases, as in all cases, is to dwell in God's Presence through worship and adoration in the midst of whatever we are going through. In doing so, His Presence with us will fulfill His purposes and fulfill the written promises of His Word whatever they are and whether or not we understand them.** (In fact, I believe that it is through this means that we come into better understanding of His Word).

Within these afflictions, we can stand on His promise that He will work wondrous new things in us, and, when we accept and expect that, his overwhelming grace (in pouring out His Presence and moving us into new ministry and understanding) completely supersedes any fear, dread, or even wondering over whether or not we will be healed. It no longer becomes the issue. When I experience His Presence in the midst of my praise, all questions about healing fall away and become totally insignificant. And I will always remember that the sufferings of this world are nothing compared to the glory that awaits us!

◆ ◆ ◆

Questions for Meditation or Group Discussion

(Note: In discussing this chapter within a group study, I would encourage the facilitator to avoid questions that argue one view of healing versus another. I do not believe it would be an edifying discussion, which is why I struggled before deciding to include this chapter in the book. If you feel you must, then I encourage you to determine first whether or not your group is of one mind on the question. It is my desire that readers concentrate on how one should respond to affliction regardless of one's position on healing.)

1. What does it mean to pray *"in Jesus' Name"*? Do you feel we need to take the words more seriously and be careful to use them correctly? What gives us the privilege of praying

in His Name? Does it matter what we are praying for when we do so?

2. In the question section of chapter 4, we asked, "Have you come to the point that, regardless of the degree of hardship or affliction in your life, the knowledge and experience of His Presence with you is blessing enough, no matter how the hardship plays out?" If you have come to this point, or if you want this to be true in your life, on what should your prayers be focused in the midst of your hardships and afflictions?

6

Moving toward His appointed ministry for you within times of affliction

In this book, I have tried to express the tremendous blessing that the Lord has brought to my life through this affliction of fatigue, depression, and brain cancer and through my response of praise within the affliction. I have spoken of the wonderful ministry opportunities to believers and to non-believers, but particularly of the way that people have been encouraged and set free to praise God in their afflictions. In this chapter, I want to deal with the more permanent nature of building ongoing ministry and operating properly within the Body of Christ as the Lord has appointed us. My affliction has given me fresh insight into this issue that is so critical for every Christian.

I cannot emphasize enough the main theme of this book—that, when God allows affliction, it is through the affliction itself and our proper response to it that the Lord brings the blessings He has designed for us. And these blessings are good and permanent and serve as seeds for further blessing. The blessings are in ministry within the Church and to the world as the Lord anoints us and we see Him bearing fruit in other peoples' lives through us. You see, if my blessing had been a miraculous and medically-evident cure, then I would simply have had a wonderful testimony that may have encouraged me for a while and ministered to others for a time after the event. But I know from my personal experience that, even though I would remain well-practiced at telling the story, the experience itself would grow stale over time and would have less and less impact in my life if not continually shored up by on-going miraculous experiences. I am glad that the Lord has not worked in that way in me. I have no evidence of any cure in my case (beyond the fact of my survival so far), and my rejoicing in the midst of an on-going terminal prognosis has continued to bring more and more blessing that is building a new and fresh ministry foundation in my life.

Fundamentally, we must first understand that the Lord has chosen specific ministry gifts for each of us. These gifts are designed to fit within our sphere of fellowship to produce a healthy Body of Christ that is ministering the Word in our communities and ministering to the needs of the Body (*I Corinthians 12-14*). This sphere of influence is usually our church. I am retired military and served on active duty for 22 years. We moved 9 times during that period and were members of many different churches of several conservative, evangelical, protestant denominations (very active in multiple ministries and almost always serving on the ruling body of the church as an ordained elder or deacon). I am fairly experienced in "church", and that experience tells me that close to 95% of Christians in church don't have a clue what ministry gifts the Lord has appointed to them. This, I believe, is simply a lack of intimacy with the Lord—another major theme of this book. But I want to share my experience with moving into a better understanding of my gifts through this affliction (because I have been part of this 95%).

The on-going search for ministry: Assessing our appointed place

Most of us who have been in church for a while are familiar with spiritual gift "tests". These are tools that present a long series of questions that you must answer on a number scale that expresses to what degree you would rather do one thing versus another, or how strongly you feel about things, or how comfortable you are in certain situations, etc. Usually, the answers are then aligned in a certain manner that allows a cumulative or average scoring against the dozen or more spiritual gifts listed in scripture. The intended use of these tests is to draw your attention to those gifts receiving the highest score as evidence of the kind of church ministry into which the Lord may be calling you. Some programs combine a spiritual gifts test with other measures such as personality tests, assessments of your talents (what you're physically good at, distinguished from spiritual gifts), and other more subjective measures like your expressions of what you feel strongly about. I have taken these tests many times in different forms over the years. Prior to my recent afflictions that are motivating this book, I consistently concluded the following things from these tests:

1. that I had no strong *relational* gifts because I was a strong introvert, always uncomfortable trying to relate one-on-one with people (although *exhortation* usually scored about mid-range);

2. that *prophecy* and *teaching* always scored the highest (by far) among all other gifts, so my ministry must lie in those areas; and

3. that I had absolutely no capability for doing anything creative or helpful with my hands, hence it was clear I was not appointed to a large array of ministries depending on that ability.

I formed a rather strong mental attitude about these things over the years. I accepted the above conclusions as making perfect sense. I struggled for years trying to casually relate to people in a way that would promote good friendships, but it always resulted in my getting exhausted and people tending to look toward others to talk with in order to avoid the discomfort of trying to make conversation with me. After a while, I stopped worrying about it and stopped trying to behave in a way that was contrary to my personality and beyond my reach. After all, it wasn't that people didn't like me; I had a good reputation in the church, and most considered themselves my friend. They just knew not to try to make casual conversation with me because I was no good at it. Good conversations came only when there was a serious discussion on a serious topic like a good scripture debate, or an evolution-creation argument, or subtle intrusion of Humanism into our Christian culture ("prophetic" topics that could be expounded upon with good "teaching"). The fact that I could talk prolifically and hold someone's attention on these topics was consistent with my high-ranking gifts. I was never clear how a gift of prophecy would be worked out in ministry (of course, some claim to have a clear understanding of this), but I always took on adult teaching as a primary ministry (which is consistent with the secular profession I ultimately chose as an *educator*). I taught classes that stuck strictly to the scripture (studying books of the Bible). I taught them in such a way as to lead the class in an established outline consistent with the message I felt the scripture was putting forth, so that I could hold the class discussion within the bounds in which I was confident. This allowed me to come to my intended conclusion (while avoiding any relational issues that might come up in the discussion of that particular scripture). I was comfortable with this kind of teaching, and my classes always had loyal members with consistent attendance. Everything seemed to be in place, but I always had a sense that I was waiting for something to happen—waiting for real anointed ministry to break forth.

I was involved with many other ministries as well; the most time-consuming were usually in church governance as a member of the Board of Deacons or Ruling Elders or Ruling Council or whatever that church called it. Leadership always rated high on my spiritual gift tests (upper third). But I always seemed to be in the middle of controversy when in these positions. I would usually defend the pastor on bold ministry initiatives that the other leaders felt were out of bounds, or I would challenge a practice within the church's operations that I felt was contrary to good order within the guidelines of scripture. These issues were usually contentious—the unavoidable consequence of good leadership, I would argue to myself. I would often prevail in these issues and lead the church along a different path in those areas only to find that there was no clear ministry fruit in the action that warranted the degree of controversy imposed. I was an effective leader at work, but it did not seem that the Lord was anointing me for leadership within the Church.

We moved to our current church when I retired from the military and took on a new career. This church takes more to heart the scriptural exhortation to thoroughly test men before appointing them to such positions (*I Tim 3:10*). Plus, it was a large church in which I could serve without pressure of being called to serve on the governing body. Therefore, I was not thrust right away into a ministry I was not called to. I found that this was a huge relief and that my heart was really not in church governance. This, coupled with my not seeing any real ministry in the past in that area, allowed me to conclude I was not called into that kind of service. This, of course, was a prelude to my questioning whether or not there was real ministry taking place in *any* of my ministry involvement; and this led to my dropping all of my ministries (except my Sunday School class) in the midst of my depression, as I described in chapter

1. But when I turned and thanked God for the affliction that was upon me and entered into intimate praise in the midst of it, ministry finally broke forth, and I gained important insight on seeking one's spiritual gifts and ministry within the Body.

It's the Fruit; not the Assessment

Not long after the terminal prognosis and my new-found intimacy in worship and the beginning of fresh daily ministry opportunities, I took yet another spiritual gifts assessment seminar at the church that went several weeks in-depth. I had signed up for it back in my depression, before anything new had started in my life (God-ordained, I believe). The results were very interesting (unlike all the previous experiences). Here is part of the overall summary I compiled at the end of the seminar (highlights refer to changes from previous tests):

Moving toward His appointed ministry for you within times of affliction

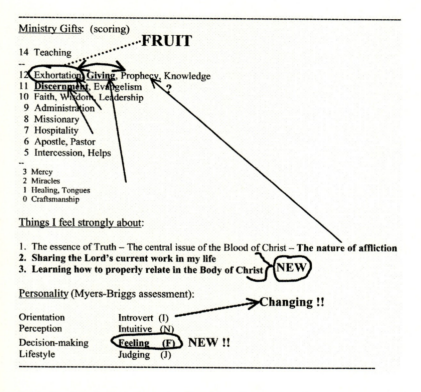

It is absolutely no surprise that "craftsmanship" remains at the very bottom. "Teaching" now rises to the very top, but my teaching over the few months just prior to this assessment had been focused on drawing out from scripture the new things God was showing me in rejoicing amidst affliction (reflecting more the message that I now had a passion for and not necessarily an anointing in teaching). (I relate this more to prophecy than teaching). But look how "exhortation" has risen to the same level from below along with "discernment" (which never ranked high) and along with "giving" (which always ranked near the bottom!). I had a new passion for sharing the kinds of things that are in this book. And in every opportunity given to me to minister since "the change", *exhortation* was the area where the Lord was clearly producing fruit through me (real, tangible fruit where I could stand and boldly say, "The Lord is bearing that fruit in this person's life through what He is doing in me").

As for teaching, I was still losing the motivation to teach (that is, I was unmotivated to prepare), yet the Lord blessed the teaching time by using me in the area of exhortation, again from my personal experience. If we are becoming intimate with the Lord, He shapes our ministries regardless of the positions we hold (and we should be patient in moving our positional responsibilities within the church until the Lord gives the explicit opportunity). He can use the anointing we have been given wherever we are.

With every instance of ministry opportunity, I formed a greater resolve toward another new passion—*relating to individuals in the Body* to facilitate this ministry. I felt the Lord clearly telling me that I could no longer use my introverted personality as an excuse not to relate. I was being called to relate, and, I believe, I am being taught that we are <u>all</u> called to relate. Many have approached me lately and commented that I seem less reserved. I look forward to going to church and talking with people now (I actually have a list of topics that would make good edifying conversation, and I always seem to have an opportunity to provide real ministry in these encounters). Supporting this is the amazing change in my Meyers-Briggs personality assessment in the area of decision making. I'm actually turning into a "feeling" kind of guy instead of a "thinker" (like I always have been). I will now tend to make decisions on the basis of how the decision will affect people rather than on the pure analytical logic that used to be the only criteria for me. I'm becoming *sensitive* to people.

I shared some of these things with my friend Sue (my radiation oncology nurse). She began to nod her head more as I went along (apparently understanding perfectly what I was describing). She said the Lord was preparing me for a ministry of *encouragement*. That was exactly what I had been sensing, and I suddenly felt as if I was finally being fitted rightly into the Body of Christ.

Here was the clincher, however. During the time I was going through this ministry gifts assessment and pondering what the Lord was doing with my personality, I attended a conference where the pastor who had declared my healing was teaching and ministering (I mentioned this in the last chapter). As he declared (among other things) that I would be a great preacher, the prophecy struck home with me and agreed with my heart (although I was not clear as to what form this "preaching" would take or what it meant to be "great"). As I continued to sit on the floor after his prayer over me, a lady (whom I didn't know but who is now my good friend Marge) remained and continued to pray for me. Later, still on the floor, this lady spoke an amazing thing to me. She said that the Lord "delighted in my personality and enjoyed being in <u>my</u> presence". (Of course, I realize that this is true for all of us, but it is awesome to hear it spoken). I approached her after the service and asked her to speak this again so I could be clear. She confirmed what she said and also shared that she had wanted to express something else but held back because "men often don't like to hear such things". She said that she felt a *tenderness* and *gentleness* in me as part of what the Lord delighted in! I was blown away and greatly humbled. I shared with her that I, indeed, felt that the Lord was growing that in me and that I was struggling with the whole issue of personality and how I had been using my personality as an excuse for insisting where I was not called to minister—that the Lord was now correcting me and moving me to a more fit place within the Body. This confirmation ministered to both Marge and me.

Now the point I am making is this. These changes in me did not start, and I did not begin seeing new avenues of ministry and long-term ministry gifts within the Body until <u>*after*</u> the Lord starting bearing fruit in those areas. They were released in my life when I responded to the affliction I was in by thanking Him and praising Him *in the midst of the affliction* and for what He wanted to do *through* the affliction. Only then did the ministry assessment test results change in a way that was not only consistent with specific ministry gifts but was also confirming the areas in which the Lord was already bearing fruit!

I wrote to my friend who was the facilitator of this ministry seminar, and I put it like this:

"I just finished addressing a group of about 50 believers here at work on the subject of how to respond to affliction & hardship and how to expect God to move within these things to reveal one's place in ministry within the Body. Near the end, I presented a one-page summary of my personal results from the seminar. I used it to demonstrate how these results change over time as the Lord effects changes in your life in response to our obedience in moving forward in the ministries He lays right in front of us. For example, my summary demonstrates that my M-B personality scores are changing consistent with a real sense of God changing my personality. My heart passions have expanded over the past 2 years, and unexpected spiritual gifts (that used to be ranked low) are now ranking much higher, consistent with the kind of ministry that the Lord is laying before me and in which He is bearing fruit. The seminar results are a changing landscape that changes faster the more responsive we are to further growth in the ministries that He selects for us. My perspective now is that, if one is not already seeing how the Lord is developing a ministry in one's life, the seminar material will not catalyze that. In fact, it might be misleading because the landscape hasn't yet been transformed!

"My message to people these days emphasizes the critical importance of building a foundation of daily praise in your life. Being filled with His Presence is foundational to effectual ministry. When He inhabits our praise, His Presence allows us to see the ministry opportunities that He sets before us, and we joyfully move forward in them and see His bearing fruit in other peoples' lives through us. It is this experience that primarily points us to our appointed direction of ministry. The seminar's benefit to me was as a tool to demonstrate how the Lord was transforming me after I responded to ministry opportunities (interactions with people, not filling church positions). It served as a confirmation, not an initial direction finder.

"For example, had I taken the seminar 3 years earlier (and I have done so piece-meal in different forums), I would have concluded that my ministry was to teach the Truth in clear and logical terms, so that others could be equipped to give an account in the world. I should practice this in teaching forums that are clear and straight-forward and that minimize the need to relate individually with people since I am not equipped or called to that. My high-ranking gifts (teaching, prophecy, knowledge) as well as my passion, talents, and personality would have all supported this. But, even though my profession involves teaching, and I have decades of experience in teaching adults at church, I don't feel I have ever really been anointed in that kind of ministry (although I wanted to be). Now, <u>after</u> the Lord began leading me into something fresh (derived from exercising praise and rejoicing in affliction) and after He demonstrated real ministry fruit in what He laid before me, the seminar results changed in a confirming way. Exhortation (which had always scored medium high) was the area that the Lord demonstrated in my life. Gifts such as 'discernment' and 'giving' bubbled up from the lower ranks. I suddenly had new passions for sharing my personal experiences and for learning how to better relate within the Body. <u>And</u> my personality scores changed (consistent with a real sense that I was a different person)—becoming a 'feeling—sensitive' person instead of the 'logical—thinking' person I always used to be. Furthermore, I became particularly impressed that aspects of my introverted nature needed to be changed in order to realize full potential in ministry. And the Lord is bringing that about."

This is the most exciting aspect of what the Lord is doing in me. I have a confidence that I will not only be blessed by ministry opportunities as I continue to rejoice in my affliction but that these opportunities will increase in the long term as I see and accept the role the Lord is granting me in the overall ministry of the Body of Christ. It is a wonderful confirmation that He is sovereign over my life and is placing me fitly and rightly among His children in ministry. This is the blessing He desires to give all of His children, and it is most certainly available to all. For me, it broke through in the midst of affliction; and if you are going through hard times right now, don't waste the opportunity for the Lord to enrich your life beyond what you have imagined. Thank Him and praise Him in the midst of the affliction and enter a new era of intimacy with the Father. **Use the affliction as an opportunity for praise!**

Then, let Him demonstrate ministry in you and show you where He has placed you among His children.

◆ ◆ ◆

Questions for Meditation or Group Discussion

1. Do you have a clear sense of what ministry gift (or gifts) the Lord has granted you within the Body of Christ? If not, why not? If so, how did you receive this sense? Is your understanding of your gifts consistent with real ministry fruit that the Lord is granting in other people through you?

2. If you do not have a clear sense of where the Lord wants to bear ministry fruit in your life, what practical steps do you think you might take to get in-the-know on this? Does it involve cycling through all the ministry positions available in your church to see what happens, or is there a more appropriate and efficient way?

3. In my case, I attribute my new ventures into realizing ministry fruit in my life to my response to affliction. What other means might the Lord use in your life to bring you into new understanding of the spiritual gifts He has already given you?

7

Expecting and desiring God's continued work in growing your ministry (The blessing of affliction)

To close this book, I want to express some summary thoughts to give more substance to the overall message I am trying to speak. As I closed the last chapter, I encouraged you to "let Him demonstrate ministry in you". This, taken by itself, is rather empty encouragement—at about the same level as someone exhorting us to "*have faith*" (as if that was a novel idea and we could try that for a change!). Something has to happen to allow the Lord to demonstrate ministry. We don't just sit around and meditate and ask for the Lord to "reveal" His appointed ministry. There is action involved. Yet, it is not very efficient (nor according to God's plan) that we jump into various ministry positions in church in a blind search for God to demonstrate His ministry power when we finally accidentally land on the right ministry position (assuming there is a "position" in your church that is well suited to your appointed ministry). Furthermore, it is not always efficient (or in God's plan) that we search for His ministry power by taking tests to determine our spiritual gifts before we have even seen evidence of them (as I discussed in the last chapter). So, what's the secret?

Purpose in our affliction

It is my belief that the Lord unilaterally brings change into our lives as a platform from which He desires to bring forth powerful ministry through us. These changes are usually uncomfortable and uninvited. They may take the form of significant hardships and trials to which we must (in one way or another) respond. We can respond with discouragement, asking God why He allowed it or why we can't seem to have the faith to "defeat" it; or we can acknowledge that God has provided (allowed, permitted,...whatever) the hardship as part of His grace in providing that missing element that brings an outpouring of ministry from our lives, brings confidence in the gifts that He is clearly demonstrating in us, and builds "faith" in our lives based on what we have *seen* the Lord *do* in our lives.

This is a principle that escaped me until I was 50 years old. I spent over half a lifetime pursuing a lifestyle of busy schedules dictated by my job and by my church, achieving a good reputation before men but never really seeing the joy of the Lord's ministry to others *through* my life. It feels like such a waste, and I see Christians everywhere in that same place. I view it as a tragedy, and I feel an unction to talk about it and declare the new thing the Lord has shown me.

We do not have the right (as God's children) to expect and demand lives that are free from hardship and affliction. On the contrary, we not only experience everything that goes with living in this corrupt world, but, as we respond correctly to affliction, we will get a lot more hardship than others because the world will begin to hate us just as it hated Him (*John 15: 18-19*). This is a blessing! We don't have to sit around pondering or reasoning out what the Lord wants to do in our lives. We have ample opportunity to respond in very real and tangible and practical ways to the hardships that beset us all the time! It is through these responses that the Lord does things in our lives that we have been pleading with Him to do! The response is simple obedience to a straight-forward command of the scripture (as we always thought it ought to be): "Consider it all joy, my brethren, when you encounter various trials, knowing that the testing (*trying*) of your faith produces endurance. And let endurance have its perfect result, so that you may be perfect and complete, lacking in nothing." (*James 1:2-4, NAS*)

I further believe that this is the manner by which the Lord continually builds us up—foundation upon foundation. I first experienced the hardship of exercise intolerance, chronic fatigue, and depression with the ensuing breakthrough of the discovery of thanksgiving, praise, and joy in response. This, in turn, prepared me to experience the hardship of the death sentence with an eleven month prognosis, the strenuous effort of putting my affairs in order, and the gut-wrenching emotions of my family. The correct response, now learned through experience with a measure of faith built into my life, brought significantly greater understanding of the Lord's Grace and wonderful purposes, greater ministry through my life, and even deeper faith and vision for further ministry. Moreover, he has spared my life for 17 months (6 months beyond expected life as of this writing) without my even asking or thinking about conjuring up enough faith for that to happen. You see, I have just come to believe through my experience, and through what I have seen the Lord do, that I will not die soon but will have much more opportunity to experience more hardship and affliction as a foundation for even more abundant living and ministry as He has promised. Praise God!

The wonderful thing about this is that you do not have to grow to some new level of faith to begin such a journey. You don't have to be trapped for years trying to reason it out or waiting for the Lord to "move" or just assuming that you don't "have what it takes". We all have hardships in our lives, and the opportunity to move straight into what the Lord has stored up for you is right in front of you. Thank Him and praise Him *in the midst of the affliction* (even if you have not learned and do not yet have "faith" that He will move—that's not the point and that is not required). Just thank Him and praise Him in the affliction and watch what He does with it. If He doesn't do something new and fresh and wonderful in your life in response, then you can contact me and bring correction to my teaching!

Again, I may have experienced a breakthrough that started a new phase of growth in my life, but that was not God's ultimate purpose. He works at the foundations, building lasting things in our lives that serve as platforms for further growth well beyond our imagination. This takes time and a great deal of patience on our part. If we form our own agenda as to what the Lord is doing in our affliction (such as working toward taking authority over it in every case to remove it), we will experience a lot of discouragement and frustration. Ours is simply to seek His Face daily and recognize what He places before us in ministry and growth (and not to look for what we want to come before us). When I learned to enter into intimate worship in the midst of my afflictions, I found that the Lord laid ministry opportunity before me every day. He always brought someone to me who needed to hear what He was doing in my life and how that applied to their own situation. There was always a moment of decision whether or not to move forward in obedience to the calling of that moment, but it was really very easy to do so because of the intimacy I was experiencing in my daily worship. Inhibitions no longer had any strength or power to hold me back. That aspect of it gets easier even though the nature of the challenges and hardships may get more rigorous. But as we move forward step by step, the new and fresh joy in the Lord sufficiently overcomes the increased rigor of the hardships, and we can move into new and glorious realms of ministry and faith (like we have seen in others but never found ourselves). The affliction we are currently experiencing is not the last one. We must expect further hardship and affliction with joy and without fear and learn the nature of the Sovereign Hand of God and His wonderful purposes in our lives. **It's not about removing the hardship and returning us to the place of comfort where we were; it's about moving us to the next hardship in building the abundant life.**

Boldness in our appointed ministry

I have always enjoyed reading about Amos when he prophesied against the king of Israel (*Amos 7:10-17*). The king told him to return to his land and prophesy there. Amos responded that he was not a prophet there but had been called by God to prophesy to Israel. He boldly stood his ground, being confident in his appointed ministry. I believe that if we boldly declare the ministry that we have seen the Lord perform in us, then this ministry is more firmly built in our hearts, our faith in God's Hand grows, and He is enabled to confirm us and grow us into deeper insight regarding our appointed ministry.

From I Corinthians 12, we can confidently say that all Christians have at least one ministry gift and that it is not appropriate to assume that anyone has all of the gifts (assuming they can be enumerated). We have latitude in the scripture, however, to allow that some or many of us have more than just one gift. It is also reasonable to assume (as we have observed) that anyone can minister in a certain way in a given situation even though that particular ministry gift does not normally characterize that person's primary ministry. But God uses affliction to build us up properly within the Body. We must give honor to what the Lord does when we praise Him in our afflictions and declare what he is doing. It is not random; He has long term purposes in it. As I have journaled my daily experiences over the last two years, I have clearly seen the fruit of a ministry of encouragement being born in my life. This allows me to be more aware of ministry opportunity when the Lord brings it before me and allows easier obedience. The Lord wants us to see, understand, and boldly declare our appointed ministry to be more effective in growing in it and to be an example among believers in finding their own ministry. Now, when I say boldly declare, I don't mean running around the church advertising our gifts. I mean agreeing with the Lord on what He has produced in us and where it is going in future ministry. The Lord will bring to us those who need to benefit from our ministry gift, but it weakens the Body when that person is brought before us and we don't recognize the opportunity because we have not planted in our hearts the ministry that the Lord has chosen to build in us and has already demonstrated in us. Boldness in our hearts opens the door to deeper praise and deeper opportunity for growth.

It is OK to have uncertainty about our calling as long as we do not ignore what the Lord is telling us in the fruit He continually bears. At some point, we must begin to accept the kind of fruit He is bearing through us and to become more expectant that He will continue what He has begun by looking for opportunities to exercise that kind of ministry and walk into them (even with less than full confidence). Later, when He has confirmed our response by continued and more powerful ministry fruit, we need to declare more boldly what the Lord has chosen to do in us and regard it as our particular anointing. Again, this journey begins when we take on a new perspective concerning our hardships and afflictions and praise the Lord in the midst of them. Never lose sight of this principle! Disappointment and frustration in our afflictions denies God's purposes and bars Him from moving us forward in His perfect plan for us.

The problem of physical affliction (healing from disease)

One of the problems that I must continually deal with is the pressure within the church to declare my own healing; that is, when I speak of my experience to church gatherings, people expect me to declare that I have been healed in Jesus' name, and the message they hear, instead, is quite different. Most are blessed by the message and try to talk with me afterwards to express this. There are a few, however, (who usually do not impose themselves on the moment) who feel I am missing the boat and not claiming what the Lord "promises" in healing His children. I devoted chapter 5 to this issue.

I have been suggesting to people that the Lord does not intend to give me a clear sign of intended healing but, instead, only indirect signs of preparation for ministry. I struggled at one

Expecting and desiring God's continued work in growing your ministry
(The blessing of affliction)

point over asking for a sign (at least for my wife Sherry's sake), and I also wondered whether or not He had already given sufficient signs, and I was just too reluctant to receive them as such. I don't concern myself with such questions anymore. I just don't sense the Lord's blessing on the questions and the wonderings. What I do see is that He is revealing things in my life that He wants to mold into a long term ministry, and it is this that I boldly declare. I have come to believe that the Lord does not want me to try to figure all this out (especially given how I am prone to insist on that). I am content to allow Him to reveal it and bring it all to light in His appointed time. My responsibility is to remain in His Presence by continual praise amidst the afflictions and the unanswered questions about it. In His Presence, all important questions are answered and all other questions just fall away!

In the midst of affliction, especially those that have no perceived end in sight or that involve terminal illness, a believer will find himself or herself in one of three places:

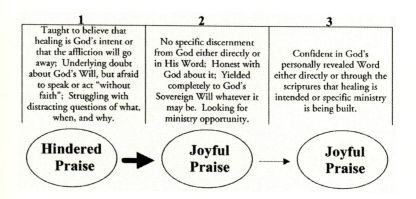

Anytime we find ourselves in the first position, we must run to the second position. If and when God chooses to move us to the third position, let us stand there with boldness. Ultimately, the critical issue is to be able to stand in His Presence with unhindered joyful praise. Then He will bring ministry into our lives and remove all questions. That is, He will build Truth into our lives surrounding the important questions, and the unimportant questions will fade away. I believe that any disagreement we may have on the physical healing of the believer is, ultimately, unimportant (even though I elected to write a chapter on the subject) as long as we agree that we should expect Him to do wonderful things in all our afflictions and we give Him praise!

It's still a battle—expect it!

Lest anyone think that I have learned a way to avoid all struggle and to be immune to any ill effects of hardship, let me assure you that is not the case. When I describe the wonderful experience of growing into an intimate worship relationship with the Lord and daily sensing His Presence and seeing His ministry amidst my hardship, one would think that I must be running to this experience every morning and that I have found a new existence free from the hindrances to spiritual growth. On the contrary, the struggle remains, and it often gets intense.

On one level, there is still the never-ending struggle of discipline within the things you know you must do. Just as we all struggle with finding daily prayer time, daily scripture time, and daily quality family time while fulfilling work responsibilities, devoting myself to a daily time of secluded intimate worship is difficult. It doesn't always happen, and when it doesn't, the price is paid in lost ministry opportunities. Either I don't see them (because I have lost a measure of intimacy with His Heart) or He doesn't bring them (for the same reason). The daily struggle doesn't get easier, and it will likely get harder.

On another level (but probably very much related), there is the greater intensity of spiritual conflict that comes with moving forward into the Lord's Heart (but especially into His appointed ministry for you). This is a topic best left to other books by those more experienced and knowledgeable than I. But I have come into a new awareness of spiritual battles that are going on. Spirits of fear, dread, disappointment, rejection, bitterness, strife, and others have beset my immediate family frequently ever since I began to praise God with new vigor in my life. The Enemy is really infuriated by it. But the Lord is merciful and loving to His children. With these attacks has come a new sense of God's sovereign authority and our power (His power) over these spirits. We have seen victory over them time and time again with a new understanding not only of the depth of the Enemy's activity against us but also of how to fight these battles with continual victory. When we become intimate with the Lord in the midst of our afflictions (instead of allowing the Enemy to discourage us), then the Enemy's attacks become more plentiful, more intense, and <u>far less effective</u>. We have renewed confidence and faith in our authority over the Enemy, and we actually experience the fact that He who is in us is greater than he who is in the world (*I John 4:4*). Expect the battle, but have no fear of it.

Rejoice always

<u>Rejoice</u> **in the Lord** *always* **(Phil 4:4)**

<u>Rejoice</u> *evermore* **(I Thes 5:16)**

In *everything* <u>give thanks</u> **(I Thes 5:18)**

Consider it *all* <u>joy</u> **(James 1:2)**

I have done absolutely nothing to deserve the huge blessings of the afflictions I have recently faced (and am facing). What a joy to be given hardship in which to discover new mysteries of our Lord's mercy and grace and power and intimate love toward us. The past year as a terminal cancer patient has been the very best year of my life. And I have learned the big secret! *Intimacy with our Lord is the key!* I wish I could describe it better than my attempt earlier in the book, but I urge you to seek it with everything you've got. I believe that the Lord has provided a special pathway for His children to find it. It is through the hardships and afflictions that give us the opportunity to thank Him and praise Him for everything He wants to do to bless us through them. Believe me! All the questions about the causes and the "why's" of our afflictions are of no account. They all go away in the joy of the Lord's Presence as He comes to us in our thanksgiving and dwells in our praise. That praise is real and genuine and effective when it is offered in full acknowledgement of our afflictions and our lack of understanding and when it is offered freely in the midst of them. Please don't waste any more time (as I wasted 50 years). Pursue this joy, victory, and continued spiritual growth by praising Him in the midst of the trial you are facing right now.

◆ ◆ ◆

Questions for Meditation or Group Discussion

1. This chapter begins by asserting that God brings uninvited change to our lives to "shake us up", if you will, toward bringing us into new levels of ministry? Do you believe this, have you experienced it, and do you desire it? Should we expect the Lord to do this, and do you feel you may have missed out on God's larger purpose in your hardships by not expecting it and by not responding to the hardship in that light?

2. Read James 1:2-4 again. Apply it to every trial you faced in your life and think about how you responded (or might have responded) in obedience to that scripture. Is there any trial in your life (past, present, or future) for which this scripture does not apply?

3. This book deals with the primary theme of responding correctly to trials in our life as the pathway for finding God's full purposes for us in ministry and abundant living. Certainly, God, in His Sovereignty and infinite ways, can use many means to accomplish this in our lives. But,

since we have been promised trials, and all of us have trials, how important is it for us to be very intimate with this particular means to grow in our faith and ministry? If we do not accept the opportunity given through our afflictions, to what extent might the Lord withhold other opportunities for breakthrough into new and fresh understanding of His appointed place for us and into understanding of His very nature?

4. Think of a hardship you are going through right now. I encourage you to praise God right now for the wonderful purposes He has in mind for you through this hardship experience. If you are in a group, declare this praise for this particular hardship openly. If you don't have a clue what the Lord is doing through it, declare that, and praise Him anyway. Do this everyday this week, assess what the Lord does with that praise, and journal about it or share it with the group the next time you meet. Challenge yourself and others to know real *intimacy* with the Lord.

Epilogue

Six months have passed since I finished the initial draft of this book, waiting for the extensive reviews to come back and making revisions here and there. As I submit the book to the publisher, it is now 23 months after my brain surgery (1 full year beyond my predicted death). The doctors now speak of ambiguity in the pathology and *probabilities* of survival. Even though I have (or had) a highly malignant cancer, I am now told that I have survived well beyond the period of likely recurrence, with a high probability of surviving the 15 year surveillance period.

It is difficult to say that I have been *miraculously* healed (no overnight disappearance of a tumor). I simply didn't die when they said I would. I am glad that I cannot point to a miraculous phenomenon—I believe it would have been distracting to what the Lord was doing in me and building in me. But I do believe that He has chosen to heal me, and I give Him all the glory for that. I never claimed that healing nor did I declare it "*in Jesus' Name*". But He did it anyway.

Does God distinguish between physical affliction and other kinds of affliction with regard to His purposes in them? Does God intend to bring physical healing to His children every time they are physically afflicted (among the many other good things He has planned)? I don't know. But I believe to focus on that as our only expectation deprives us of the full riches of God's plan for us.

I have chosen to praise Him and rejoice in Him in the midst of my afflictions (physical or otherwise) and allow Him to be sovereign in my life, revealing in His time what are the full riches of His purposes. Within this response I have experienced great ministry fulfillment and, yes, physical healing.

I encourage you in intimate praise and in rejoicing in <u>all</u> things. He intends great things for us, and He is sovereign. Let Him do so and be so in your life.

Mike Shelley
August 2004

0-595-32857-1

Printed in the United States
22877LVS00001B/1-102